1007503319

THE THEORY OF SCIENCE

A Philosophical Investigation
into the Symbolic Reduction of Experience

THE THEORY OF SCIENCE

A Philosophical Investigation
into the Symbolic Reduction of Experience

John Roscoe

The Edwin Mellen Press
Lewiston•Queenston•Lampeter

Library of Congress Cataloging-in-Publication Data

Roscoe, John, date.
  The theory of science : a philosophical investigation into the symbolic reduction of experience / John Roscoe.
      p. cm.
  Includes bibliographical references (p.   ) and index.
  ISBN-13: 978-0-7734-3609-1
  ISBN-10: 0-7734-3609-X
1. Science--Philosophy. 2. Experience.. I. Title.
  Q175.R5466 2010
  501--dc22
                                     2010022742

hors série.

A CIP catalog record for this book is available from the British Library.

The Edwin Mellen Press   The Edwin Mellen Press
        Box 450   Box 67
   Lewiston, New York   Queenston, Ontario
   USA 14092-0450   CANADA L0S 1L0

                  The Edwin Mellen Press, Ltd.
                  Lampeter, Ceredigion, Wales
                  UNITED KINGDOM SA48 8LT

            Printed in the United States of America

For Sunniva, John and Magnus.

CONTENTS

PREFACE

A book of philosophy, no matter how restricted its ostensible topic may be, must in some sense address the general problem of Philosophy; for this reason it will be helpful to make quite explicit how the present essay does just that. The philosopher (in common, of course, with all non-philosophers) makes use of language to persuade others, but no less himself, of something that seems important to him. Philosophy is inconceivable without writing, so that what he does is, more particularly, to produces arguments in the form of *texts*. The meaning any text has for its readers, and no less for its writer, is informed by those of others texts which together constitute the *context* in which it is written and read; it is precisely this context that our lexica and encyclopædias strive to capture. The text and context are produced in a certain *medium*, namely the language of writers and readers, and it is this medium that gives all the texts their meaning. It can itself, however, only be described in yet another text, a grammar of the language, employing the same medium yet again. There would, then, be an evident circularity in any attempt to explain the *meaning* of a text (and, more generally, of anything we choose to say) and this being so, the relationship of our words to the world we seek to understand becomes something ineffable. Herein lies the general problem of Philosophy. In a recent book, *The Picture Theory of Meaning*, I showed how the genesis of meaning is to be understood in terms of the natural meaning that our pictures have for human beings and the games that can be played with them. I hope I may have indicated the way to elude the circularity that I have just noted and so contributed to a solution of the problem. The present essay is intended to explain the sense in which the enterprise of Science is essentially the business of first making pictures of the world of human experience and then reducing these pictures to mathematical symbols. This not only extends the scope of the argument of the former book but also clarifies it in allowing Science to become an intelligible model for the more fundamental procedure by which human language is related to the world of Man.

The present book emerged from my seminar for doctoral candidates in the natural sciences at Stavanger University and its evolution was further stimulated by discussions in the Philosophical Forum held periodically at the sign of the Cardinal. I owe a debt of gratitude to students, colleagues and good friends at both venues, and in particular to Barbara Bauer, Rune Ingebrethsen, Knut Lunde, Bjørn Nicolaysen, Bjørn-Olav Roaldseth, Brit-Helen Russdal-Hamre and Stig Selmer-Anderssen.

Vikedal, 2010

INTRODUCTION

Viewed in the perspective of this essay Science is the quest for understanding. This will already distinguish it from the many works on the Philosophy of Science from the last century which insisted that Science is the quest for knowledge. By that was meant that the goal of scientific activity is possession of the truth which in turn meant to have written down certain true propositions. The ultimate reason for this position was that the Analytic Philosophy of the Twentieth-Century was built upon a logic of truth-values. The alternative foundation assumed here in that of primitive human meaning. The difference this makes will not emerge without a certain amount of argument but can be immediately suggested in this way: what is meant by understanding is precisely the grasping of complex meaning.

We are doing philosophy whenever we take a step back from the world and question our engagement with it. The philosophizing the scientist might do when he looks up from his notebook or laboratory bench is the subject matter of the Philosophy of Science. When the philosopher presumes to philosophize on the scientist's behalf his reflections will have to find their place as an integral part of the discipline of philosophical thought. The principal departments of this discipline are Anthropology, on the one hand, and Metaphysics on the other. Anthropology (as understood by the Philosopher) is the study of human existence, including in particular the dimension identified as ethical. Ethics is the discussion of the constraints men ought to impose upon their behaviour and its method should be noted: it intends to be rational and the matter it discusses is the systematic relatedness of certain abstractions. Metaphysics, on the other hand, is the study of the stage upon which this behaviour occurs and is typically concerned with a real stage behind that upon which it merely seems to occur. Given this characteristic preoccupation Metaphysics busies itself with the medium of human experience, that is with the mind that contains it and so with the language in which it is expressed and the rationality that is brought to bear upon that expression. Language and Logic are accordingly two of its own departments and Metaphysics, like Ethics, pursues its quest for understanding by the investigation of abstractions. Whilst its own rational method is closely related to scientific thought, it is the abstract subject matter of Philosophy that emphatically separates it from Science.

The abstractions in question are *Goodness, Justice, Beauty*, and so on, in the case of philosophical Anthropology, and *Being, Action, Meaning, Reason*, and so on, in the case of Metaphysics. Their reliance upon an appropriate development of language should be noted. The resources of a fully evolved natural language permit the recruitment of words from one syntactical category for use, usually in modified form, in another. It is only when the use of adjectives has been instituted (as of "good," and "just" in our English language) that the abstract substantives "Goodness" and "Justice" can be adopted to make ethical discussion possible, and only when the form of such words can also be given to the verbs "be," "act," "mean," "think," and so on, as "Being," "Action," "Meaning" and "Thought," that the metaphysical abstractions can become a part of rational discourse. What philosophers must never lose sight of is the origins of the meanings of their words which is why the study of Language has the central rôle it does in Western Philosophy. The history of the language of Science will be of concern to us throughout this essay, for whilst Language does not determine the content of Science, it does supply the scientist with the ultimate materials for his models and the ultimate means for their manipulation.

To identify the discussion of abstractions as the essence of philosophical thinking and to deny that Philosophy and Science are the same activity is, of course, to point to scientific subject matter as something other than abstract. However, to say that Science is non-abstract thinking would not be enough; it is not only misleading to characterize its thought as essentially *concrete* but this hardly explains why the thinking of an engineer who has a river to bridge, or a city to build, for example, is not a scientific exercise, for nothing could be more concrete than his field of activity. But in seeing, as we readily do, that the concrete thinking of an engineer is concerned with the particular application of principles that typically derive from properly scientific work, we recognize that only what is sufficiently *general* can be said to be Science.

The engineer can apply its concrete, general principles because Science works in the sense that it can inform what practical men do. That Science works in this sense might seem sufficiently to distinguish it from non scientific activity that is deliberately intended to look like Science and so is quite properly described as pseudo-science. The best counter-example might then be homeopathic medicine which has a technical vocabulary borrowed from real science and adopted to impress the ignorant rather than to facilitate the sharing of insight amongst specialists. It also has its own non-functional apparatus, inert preparations and white-coated practitioners with diplomas in Latin hanging on their walls. Whilst such charlatanry is easily rejected as being nothing more than a testimony to the prestige of genuine science, homeopathy too apparently works.

It is not pseudo-science but certain honest intellectual enterprises that put our understanding of what Science is to the test. To the least benighted of the theologians who valiantly tried to make a science out of Religion the proper way towards a definition of their illusive deity was the consideration of what it is not. The same *via negativa* would lead us in our quest to pose such questions as the following: *Why is Astrology not science? Why is Chemistry science but not Alchemy? Why is Freudian Psychology not science (or is it)? Is Darwinian thinking scientific? Is Economics?* None of these questions is easy to answer. On the other hand, there can be no questioning the credentials of Mathematical Physics, for if it is not science then nothing is; the same must be allowed to be true of Chemistry and Biology, for otherwise Science and Physics would become one and the same thing, which is not what we want to say. To reveal its true essence, those academic disciplines whose status is doubtful must be ranged against these undoubted paradigms as objects of comparison.

The claim I want to make is this: that what makes Science Science can only be *the peculiar mode of its exercise of reason*. In the sequel I shall try to substantiate it in the manner of a philosopher by considering the abstractions that seem to be involved. I shall be guided by the notion that I have tried to justify above that Science seems to be an intellectual exercise concerned with concrete entities and leading to general conclusions which typically have the potential to inform our practical doing. A successful identification of the peculiar mode in question would allow the status of problematic cases to be decided. Successful demarcation is thus the goal but that does not determine the methodology of our enquiry. This will emerge by reviewing the plan of the present essay which is as follows.

My *first chapter* is entitled **Intuition**. What we understand by the abstract term "intuition" is the acquisition of a mental view which—before we are troubled by our philosophizing—can seem to be the *immediate* apprehension of what is real. The first task for a philosophy of Science is to dispel this misconception by proposing that the only way in which anything is *present to us* is in its being *represented by us*. In less abstract terms the philosopher's claim is, then, that we only *see* what we might also have *pictured*. Once this is grasped the notion of immediate contact with reality has to be replaced by that of one mediated by the pictures that we can make. This already compromises the view that Science is concerned with what is true, for to be "true" could only mean to be faithful to a Reality which is now seen to be beyond at least immediate apprehension. The most familiar medium of human representation and the one in which the results of scientific investigation are presented is that of *Language*. It is of vital importance on account of its implication in the process by which intuition is transformed into understanding. The second task of this chapter is, then, to uncover the workings of language by distinguishing, on the one hand, the *semantic* apparatus by which words derive their meanings from natural forms of picturing and, on the other, the *syntactical* apparatus by which complex meanings are derived from simpler ones.

The title of my *second chapter* is **Insight**; the meaning of this term—one crucial to my argument—is that which is seen with the Mind's metaphorical eye when we peer into what is hidden beneath the surface of the things that arouse our curiosity. The approach adopted here is to engage the reader in a certain amount of experimental play with triangles and squares to underline the rôle of constructing and manipulating representations and, in particular, the exploration of their symmetry in the reasoning that issues in the *laws* traditionally seen as the goal of scientific investigation. A proper understanding of what such a law is begins to emerge with the recognition of features that are invariant across all the members of an ensemble of different representations.

But no insight becomes a law until it has been warranted as such. My *third chapter*, **Reason**, is accordingly concerned with the employment of the characteristically human power of mind in self-consciously regulating its own action. A similar approach is adopted here but this time the experimental play upon which it is focussed is with counters, *i.e.* with undifferentiated representations of things for counting. What can then be explained is the manner in which the self-conscious business of constructing proofs emerges as warranty is sought for what we seem to discover about the possible and impossible geometrical arrangements of different numbers of things. There is a variety of intellectual equipment deployed in this enterprise, *viz.* the different modes of rational argumentation: *analogy*, *induction* and *deduction*. To be sure that we are not deceived in their employment the logician provides symbolic models of them to which we require individual passages of argumentation to conform (the prototype of these canonical models is Aristotle's Syllogistic which, despite its fame, is hardly of anything other than antiquarian interest and does not concern us here). To be sure that these *syntactical* entities are consistent and so will not lead us astray the logician provides them with a *semantics* of their own. But the critical investigation of these models reveals that there is more to rational thinking (and so, in particular, to scientific thinking) than argumentation in any mode; the rest of this essay is an attempt to make clear what that is.

The chapter that follows is given the title **Representation**. We have already indicated that what we want to be understood by "representation" is something that makes something else present to us (as her portrait does a distant friend). The whole argument of this essay depends upon an acknowledgement that the scientist's primary form of representation is not any text he may compose—although, as we shall see, that too has its indispensable rôle—but the *model* he constructs in his quest for understanding. The object of this *fourth chapter* is to demonstrate the kind of model that is of use to him and to explain why it should be so. The models in question are *material objects;* they can be said to be *semantic* rather than *syntactical* entities in that they give their meanings to symbols rather than being composed of them. We began this *Introduction* by assigning everything *abstract* to the province of Metaphysics and nothing of this nature—*Continuity*, for example, or *Space*, *Time*, or *Life*—can be dealt with scientifically until a material model of it is available (although only pictures of these models may actually be produced, so that they remain in that sense merely imaginary constructs). When no such model could be constructed or even consistently imagined—as in the case of a completed *infinity* of discrete entities—then we are confronted by something beyond the metaphysical frontier of the province of science.

The models produced by the scientist are the objects of his quest for insight. The particular form of insight that he is seeking is the discovery of pattern in what is presented by his models and the pattern that above all engages his attention is that of **Symmetry**. Our curiosity easily rests when we recognize it, so that it is its absence or breach that challenges our understanding. Indeed, scientific understanding can seem to be the uncovering of latent symmetry in the world of experience and many instances are produced to corroborate this claim.

"Symmetry" is the title of the *fifth chapter*. The chapter that follows closely on, my *sixth* then, is entitled **Symbolization**. Leafing through it, the too casual reader would find many diagrams that might seem to be more at home in a book written for mathematicians; this impression, however, is wrong. What I do in this chapter is essential to a proper grasp of the nature of scientific understanding: I exhibit the semantic basis of important fragments of the symbolic language of the mathematician. I start with the natural numbers, the numbers with which we count, and then progress to such unnatural numbers as 0, -1, and ∞ and am particularly concerned to explain the geometrical diagrams which supply the original semantics for the calculus.

The reason why the reader could not be spared all this becomes apparent in our seventh and *final chapter*; its title is **Theory** and its content a careful analysis first of the *Euclidean paradigm* for systematic intellectual work and then of the *Newtonian Paradigm* for the particular intellectual work of the scientist which has so often been confounded with it. What emerges is the rôle in the latter of the construction of models of a peculiar kind, *viz.* ones whose constituents can be made to correspond with elements of the semantic foundation of items in the mathematician's repertoire of symbols. This having been done the *Syntactico-Semantic Conception of Science* can finally be explained and compared and contrasted with the conceptions it is intended to supersede. The claim put forward for the reader's verdict is that only such a conception—under which *a scientific theory is a presentation of warranted conclusions drawn from the symbolic manipulation of empirical intuition*—can adequately explain the applicability of theory in the world of experience.

INTUITION

Representation

1. Our scientific quest for understanding has led us to a way of life that just about everybody on the planet now seeks to emulate, so that it is hardly possible to travel anywhere that is not modern and westernized by any other route than that of colourful imagination. We would, however, grasp the particularity of modernity most dramatically were we able to travel to the dawn of humanity. It is the exercise of imagining the unquestionably human that is as *primitive* (by which we mean, of course, as unlike our existence) as we can manage that teaches us as much as we can ever know of what human beings are and what they are about. What is, then, the limit of what we can imagine?—We have difficulty imagining the non-human animals from which we must have evolved going silently about their lives, but we need not imagine them talking: it is enough that we imagine them chattering like monkeys. It is harder, however, not to imagine them making pictures, at the very least gesturing with their hands in the empty air. *Pictures* (the traces of such gesturing) are the earliest remains of unquestionably human existence that survive; in having the naturalness that language lacks, picture-making is also the most primitive manifestation we can imagine of what we call *Mind*. A human picture is a picture for all humans, whereas a word is a meaningless sound for those who have not acquired the language to which it

belongs: the difference is that between *natural endowment* and *culture*, although it is part of our common human endowment that we, unlike other creatures, can accomplish the cultural achievement of acquiring a language.

We look at the painting on the walls of a cave made, so we are told, thirty or forty thousand years ago and cannot doubt that their makers were people like ourselves albeit not yet cultivated to any appreciable degree. Why did they make them?—The most general answer we can propose is this: that they were made to *represent* (*i.e.* to *re-present*) within the human space of the cave what was *present* somewhere outside. They must, we feel, have represented it in other ways that leave no traces for the palæo-anthropologist: we can hardly doubt that they threw animal skins over their shoulders and danced about the cave trumpeting and howling in imitation of mammoths and sabre-toothed tigers. *We suppose that what is present to humans (the forest and its animals in the case of our imagined tribe) is also to some degree present to other creatures. But only we humans* **represent** *what is present.*

Understanding

2. In their caves these ancestors of ours represented for themselves what was beyond its walls. They painted—and what was gore and charcoal became, for example, a bison. This is what is distinctively human: for us, but not for any other form of life we have encountered, *things present can make-present things other than themselves*. Without this potential for other-being, there would clearly be no representation. I want to say that acts of representation and understanding are one and the same. Clearly, representation is *sufficient* for understanding, because a man cannot put more into a picture than he has understood (this is why the Renaissance began as it did with the picture-making of Leonardo and his friends); it is another question, one with which we shall soon be concerned, whether it is also *necessary*, whether, that is, a man has understood anything that he has not represented to himself. However this may be, we do not find in our ancestral caves any very profound quest for understanding. We do not find, for example,

paintings of men studying the paintings on their wall, and certainly not ones of themselves painting them. However, just to consider that such pictures might have been there is to see how much perplexity—the stimulus to the quest—picture-making could foster. *As the only creatures that* represent, *only we can seek to understand what is present and only we have any capacity for* **understanding**.

Thinking

3. We are not cavemen; although we do still make pictures—especially for the aesthetic (rather, that is, than explanatory) qualities that make them works of art—we suppose our primary mode of engagement with the world to be a mental activity called "**thinking**" that is very like the silent, inner utterance of words. We suppose this because, especially when we are alone or unguarded, our silent, inner words can "slip out," as we say, and become audible (and, similarly, congenitally deaf people are plausibly reported as signing to themselves when they are alone). Thinking, then, can seem to be an activity in which our words permit us to engage. But from where do these words of ours come? As we have already noted it is undoubtedly natural for humans to acquire the language of the tribe into which they are born; words, however, are not naturally meaningful. How do our tribal words come to have the meanings they do, or, indeed, any meanings at all?—How is it that we can do with them what we otherwise would have had to do with the representation that comes naturally to us of picture-making in the air or on the walls of a cave? Any attempt at explaining this ought to start with something that needs no explanation, or, at least, that cannot have one; here our capacity for making pictures will serve very well.

Semantics

4. That our experience includes *things which represent other things* (i.e. pictures) is simply what it is like to be one of us and not a non-human animal: such is our **human form of life**. What explanation could there possibly be for this?—In striving to understand ourselves it is important to distinguish what we can and

cannot imagine ourselves doing. We can imagine the pictures on the walls of the cave being lively representations of individual things, but we can also imagine them being stereotypical repetitions, each bison, for example, being drawn following one and the same schematic procedure. We can imagine the following *schema* serving for the *bison*-drawing: first a stroke for its hindquarters; next a line for its humped back; then others for its horns and head, its belly, and, finally, its legs.

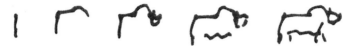

We can easily imagine our cavemen being satisfied with schematic depictions rather than the full-blooded ones we actually find in Altamira and Lascaux. Were one of these schematic depictions (say our bison) to be lifted out of a complex picture (of a bison-hunt, for example) and considered in isolation, it would still be a picture (having the natural meaning of any more full-blooded version), but—in being schematic—it would also be **the token of a type** and so apt for being used as a **word**. Here are several tokens of a type which is a word of our written language: *bison, bison, bison*; here are several tokens of a type of picture which might function in some hieroglyphic language much as the word *bison* does in ours: ♟ ♟ ♟. Schematic drawings or words categorize the things of our experience, indeed many philosophers would say that they articulate a primordial experience that would otherwise be simply an undifferentiated sameness. Thus in making this stereotypical representation such things as *bison* with their horns, humps, and so on, would have come into being as part of the world of Neolithic humanity. The most primitive style of thought of which we have any knowledge is the totemism which is clearly only made possible by the categorization of natural things that itself follows from their being given their common names, so that it is already dependent upon language.

Now, in acquiring English we had to learn to articulate many words including *bison*. How we do this is very complicated to describe, involving as it does intricate movements of the tongue and lips. In the case of our conjectural hieroglyphic language we should have to master a schema of the kind illustrated above for producing drawings that could be accepted by our fellows as tokens of their types of words. What is involved in the acquisition of our mother-tongue is somewhat similar, albeit rather harder to describe. In endeavouring to grasp what Language is, we reach no further than to the specification of rule-governed activities like this stereotypical bison-drawing—a game that we can easily learn to play. What makes us more than mere animals is that we are creatures of a kind whose form of life includes such self-contained activities (or **games,** as philosophers call them in their discussions of language).

Whereas it would not be a simple task to explain how the word *bison* comes to represent those things in the world that it does, there would be little need for explanation were this type of drawing the word of some language. And indeed, were there such a language, we could go a considerable way towards explaining the meaningfulness of the English word by saying that it was conventionally co-ordinated by English speakers with this picture-word. To explain how the words of a language have the meanings they do is to give a **semantics** for the language, so that to exhibit *bison* and its analogue ♛ together is a contribution to a semantics for the English language. If 𝓧 and 𝓦𝓦 were also words of our imaginary language, then I would be in a position to expand my English semantics to include the meanings of the words *man* and *chasing*.

In this explanation of mine I used the materials I have to hand—pen and paper—to allow *something readily understood* (the words of a purely conjectural hieroglyphic language) to represent *something very obscure* (the meaningfulness of the words of our natural tongue). I did not represent the word "bison" by exhibiting something perceptually similar to it (in the way, then, I might use the picture of a bison to represent a bison), but by exhibiting instead something that might *work* in the same way—something with which might be done what English speakers do with the word "bison." This notion of **functional sameness** is an extension to which we shall often have recourse in the sequel to the everyday meaning of "represent".

Syntax

5. In mastering such games our tribesmen would be articulating the words of the conjectural language, but this would not be sufficient in itself to make them capable of uttering meaningful sentences, for there is more to a language than is captured in the semantics of isolated words: what there is in addition is precisely what no parrot could ever grasp. The world that might be brought into being by types of schematic drawings would be nothing more than the endless change which in ours is merely the backdrop against which things of interest persist. But given the skill which our earliest ancestors also seem to have possessed, the pictures on the walls of their caves (ones of people and dogs, for example) might also have been **portraits**. They would then bring *individual* things into being (rather, that is, than undistinguished tokens) and an innovation would be required that ought perhaps to be understood as a great intellectual advance. To represent individuals *linguistically* is a new game, one that we play *with* words rather than in making them. The words we have taken into use distinguish things by their types, but given that they can be used at all for the purposes of distinction, they can also be employed to distinguish things along, as it were, another dimension. It may not be apparent in an old culture like ours with its complex history of borrowings and imitations, but that is precisely what we do in giving things their **proper names**: we take the name of a type and use it to distinguish an individual which is generally not of that type. Thus we might call a man "Wolf" or a dog "Bison." In writing English we show that we are using a word with this exceptional intention by giving it an upper-case initial. In a hieroglyphic language we might, for example, underline a schematic drawing when it was being used in this way, so that ▟ would be the name of something or somebody. It could aquire this meaning in a game in which words were associated with portraits.

Nothing that has been said so far can explain how the English sentence *A bison is chasing a man* could come to have the meaning it does. We have to consider further games that we can imagine our ancestors playing. A starting point might be a picture on the wall of a cave for which this English sentence—a sequence of English words—would supply an appropriate title.

The crucial game (in the sense insisted upon above of *self-enclosed, rule-governed activity*) would consist in extracting a sequence of schematic drawings from the picture in such a way that the picture (at least in a schematized version) could subsequently be remade by re-instating these drawings. We need not suppose that our troglodytes could articulate the rules (which, of course, as the language-less creatures they are as the game begins, they would not be able to do). In essence the game would consist in removing elements from a two-dimensional picture and making a one-dimensional arrangement of schematic versions of them. The rules might require the action illustrated to be extracted from the picture in a drawing that would serve the same purpose in the case of any picture of what would thereby become the same action (which is how we use our word "chase," for example). The games played with depictions of static things could now be played with those involved in this action; they could be removed from the reduced picture in a definite order, perhaps the active thing first and then the passive one, and the corresponding words written down. Following the rules of this game might result in the picture we have been considering being replaced by this sequence of tokens: ▜ ⸬ 𝍐. A different sequence, such as 𝍐 ⸬ ▜, would have a different meaning and, indeed, because syntax is a systematic business, we see that this would be that of a man chasing a bison.

The game instituted in our tribe might, of course, have quite different rules, so that the order could be another (for example, these sequences might as easily be ⸬ ▜ 𝍐 and ⸬ 𝍐 ▜, respectively). What is important is that the spatially organized picture has become an ordered sequence of what are essentially its own pictorial elements.

Syntactico-Semantic Integrity

6. This elementary game already has a certain complexity: schematic pictures of bison and of men running have to be replaced by static pictures of the same creatures at the same time as a token of the *chasing*-picture is incorporated into the sequence of hieroglyphic words. *Bison-* and *man-*tokens then have to be given their places in the sequence—in the order that correctly distinguishes a translation of *A man is chasing a bison* from one of *A bison is chasing a man.* To specify the order in which the rules by which such a game is played are applied is to give the **syntax** of the language, the other component of its description to put alongside its *semantics.* We have supposed the sequence of schematic pictures just considered

to be well-formed in that it does have a meaning for our players, *viz.* that naturally possessed by the picture from which it was derived. The semantics of the language is the language-making game that enables the picture to be recovered from the sentence. We see what the rules of that game will have to be: first, the *chasing*-picture will instruct the player to draw something indeterminate chasing something else; then the *bison*-picture will instruct him to make the active thing a bison; and, finally, the *man*-picture will instruct him to make the passive thing a man. **Doing** this—recovering a schematized version of the original picture—is all that could be required before we should have to say that the sentence had been understood. To credit the parrot that utters human sentences with understanding would be to imagine it doing something analogous. This suggests the strong **association between doing and understanding** to which we shall return. Our conjectural language shows us how semantics and syntax interact to become the *syntactico-semantic whole* that a language is. Without its semantics, the well-formed sequence of symbols is meaningless; without its syntax, there is no integrated complex meaning beyond the simple meanings of individual signs. This is an important clue to the proper understanding of what we call *Science*: as we shall see, there is a clear sense in which a scientific theory too is an integrated syntactico-semantic whole.

Models

7. We also find in our ancestral caves artefacts which, whilst far too crude and æsthetically unpretentious to be called sculptures, might be described in workaday language as *models* of animals and people. This word "model" is of the very greatest importance in grasping what Science is. As I have just used it (which was in one of the two relevant ways in which it can be used) the word means a plastic replica of something else, so that the model is *like* that original but, as we say, *less real*. A model bison, for example, might be a carving in bone of one of the animals which runs about in the real world. This then is an explanation of what it means for something to be **a model of** something else. But we also use the same

word in a second sense in ordinary conversation, for were I to paint your portrait, you would be **the model for** my picture. In this sense some bison encountered on the plains is the model for the bone-carving and, more generally, what we call the **real world** is the model for the pictures on the walls of our cave. In certain cases it will be possible to **compare** the picture with the model to determine how lifelike it is: were I to paint your portrait on the wall and you then came to visit my cave, for example.

But I could also paint an imaginary portrait: I could paint a picture of a person without having any model pose in front of me or anybody in particular in mind. In your portrait, you are the person shown; but who is the person shown in my fictitious portrait?—In its case *the model for the picture* exists only in being shown in the picture—it is an **artefact of my representation**. In its case there is no comparison to be made and the question of likeness has become meaningless. When the model in this second sense is not present to be compared with the model in the first sense, it can appear something ghostly and intangible: a *merely represented thing*, not something that might be chased through the forest and which might fatally turn and kill its pursuers. It does not seem to measure up to Reality but an important point for understanding the business of scientific explanation is this: simply by looking at a picture you cannot know whether or not it is merely imaginary. Nevertheless you can talk about the model for the picture: its model is *the thing shown as thought it were real*: it belongs not to *Reality* but to *modelled reality*. When we can compare the two, we hold the model up to Reality and so make a judgement of the **adequacy** of the model. In the case of a fictitious model, there is no such judgement to be made. This is what the diagram below is intended to suggest. A claim that I would make is the following, that the hieroglyphic language outlined above is a *model* of a rudimentary fragment of natural language[1]. By this I do not mean a model of any particular language (English, say), but of any human language (including, then, English). It is by

---

[1] This model is discussed at length in my *Picture Theory of Language.*

comparing what we can *do* with the hieroglyphic language with what can be done with the fragment it is intended to model that its adequacy is to be decided.

Reality   *Modelled Reality*

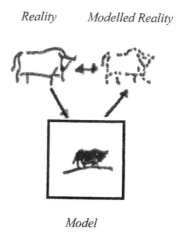

Model

You would find it odd to be told that what is real for our cavemen is precisely the world of dangerous beasts he has painted on the wall. But if you agree with my suggestion that we only **understand** what we have represented for ourselves, then things are turned upside down in just this way. We do not *understand* the un-pictured world, the world for which we have made no model (the *un-modelled world*, as it were). If there was, then, anything more to the world of language-less troglodytes beyond what is found in their pictures, it can only have been in pantomime: in gestures they made with their hands, in movements they made with their bodies and in their utterance of inarticulate sounds, of all of which, of course, no trace is left. What we have called the *Reality* that can be present to us becomes something no more solid than our representations of it. It is the pictures that are the primary reality, and what we usually call *Reality* is nothing more than what our pictures show it to be. For this reason—when we are thinking philosophically about our relationship with the world—we prefer to say that what we otherwise call Reality is **modelled reality**: the model **for** our world is the models we make **of** it.

Ampliation

8. This statement would seem *paradoxical* were it taken for a claim that *nothing is present before it has been represented*; that, however, is not what is being said. There is a clear sense in which an unrepresented bison is present to a hunter: the hunter is affected in the particular way he is as his behaviour clearly shows. But reflexion will show that without representation the bison that may be present is *not available as an object for the hunter's reason*. He cannot, for example, make any plan for its capture and slaughter, or for the sharing of its meat amongst his companions. If he makes a picture of the bison or impersonates it in any way, then what there is is not only present but also represented. His representation might then be added to those of other hunters lying in wait at some distinctive spot in the forest. As this extended representation is made, the ambush—which is not yet in progress—clearly exists only as its artefact: had it not been represented, it would not exist at all. More generally we can say that what is permitted by representation is the **ampliation**[2] of what there is. What is present but not yet represented contains within itself nothing more than its own transient individuality.

We can understand now why Language and not picture-making should be our primary mode of representation, why, that is, cavemen did not stop at the natural business of making pictures but went on to develop a language. For with Language more can be done than merely giving a picture its title. It is not just a matter of the convenience of being able to make representations in the dark or on the run: *Language enables the ampliation of representation in a way a model does not*. For, to continue with our example of the representation of an ambush, there is no way that anything other than a sentence can explain what the intended relationship is between the representations. Only with language can actors be identified and re-identified, and moved through the modalities of possibility and time.

---

[2] The *OED* declares the verb "ampliate" to be obsolete. If this be so, it certainly needs to be revived in this specific sense of "extending" or "amplifying".

Nevertheless, something is lacking in linguistic representation, something that only an iconic model can provide, which is why we so often find ourselves including pictures and diagrams in our texts. The true relationship between text and picture is more like this: only a picture has the natural meaning that constitutes understanding; our words are meaningful only because they are conventionally associated with pictures. Language enables us to do things *with* pictures, to play games with them. But when our play is done, it is still only the pictures we have then produced that *mean* anything.

Empirical Reality

9. When we are not engaged in fantasy, we suppose ourselves to be touched by Reality. In our most ordinary use of language what we intend is to allow that Reality to be the model for what we write or say. There is, however, a worry that is very deeply felt by the philosopher but which the scientist *qua* scientist cannot allow to trouble him. The philosophical disquiet is that we cannot know how like or unlike Reality our model may be, for there is no perspective available to us in which to compare the two. Indeed, many philosophers in our own time would agree with Kant that the notion of *Reality unmodelled* is not even coherent. An interesting vehicle for pondering this matter is the famous drawing associated with the name of Jastrow, a version of which appears below[3].

---

[3] Its interesting provenance is traced by W.J.T. Mitchell in his *Picture Theory* (1994). Joseph Jastrow published it in his *Fact and Fable in Psychology* in 1900. The Gestalt psychologist Köhler makes use of it as does the philosopher Ludwig Wittgenstein in his *Philosophische Untersuchungen*.

Its very disturbing property is this, that as we look at the drawing it oscillates between representing a rabbit looking to the left and a duck looking to the right. When it is the turn of the rabbit we might represent what we see by making a drawing like that on the left below which reveals the animal concealed behind the clump of grass; when it is the turn of the duck, the drawing on the right performs the same office. We might also, of course, represent it by saying either "Duck!" or "Rabbit!" The question might now be put: What is it that Jastrow's picture *really* represents—is it a duck, or is it a rabbit? And we see that there is no answer. My two drawings represent the alternatives which are, on different occasions, as different psychological events, made present to us by Jastrow's original. But there is nothing that can be said to be present independently of some representation. Bearing this demonstration in mind—and viewing the psychological curiosity as analogous with our situation as creatures perceiving the world around us—we are made wary of the notion of a Reality which is anything other than our Modelled Reality.

Such scruples would, however, make the scientist's task impossible, so he must set them to one side; the only Reality he can be concerned with is Empirical Reality—*i.e.* what seems to him simply to be there, quite independently of our thinking about it. The philosopher can have his doubts for himself; the business of the scientist is to understand **Empirical Reality** by making models of it and because of the technological mastery of it that he achieves—as though Empirical Reality were Reality *simpliciter*—the philosopher is very concerned to understand how he does it.

Lebenswelt

10. We reflect upon the history and pre-history of our species with no little complacency, for what we then seem to find in returning in imagination to our most primitive human forebears is men and women anatomically just like ourselves (and so presumably of the very same mental capacity) but with none of our understanding—or almost none, for there is a clear limit to what we can imagine human beings not having understood. Thus we cannot imagine them lacking an insight into the behaviour of their fellows, an empathetic insight of each, that is, into the **mentality** of the others. It must seem to them, as it does to us, that every other human being has certain beliefs about the way things are, about the way things ought to be, and about what needs to be done. And this being so we cannot but imagine them seeking, as we also do, to influence one another's behaviour by cajoling, suggestion or command according to relationships of power which thereby make themselves known.

But do we have to extend their lack of surprise to the world of non-human things? Must we, that is, see them largely unsurprised by what happens next, or by what follows from their own actions as they descend from their trees and set out across the savannah? Whilst lack of surprise might as readily be attributed to a flock of wolves or even an army of soldier-ants, we cannot imagine primordial human understanding as the mere *being-at-home-in-the-world* of other animals; we want to say that insofar as we imagine lousy, hirsute, stone-throwing, diseased and anxious creatures who can neither talk nor even make fire to be human at all, we have to endow them with an understanding that is quite different from mere adaptation to their environment. For they *represent* for themselves what, were they mere animals, would only be *present*, and they live in the world of their representations, their *Lebenswelt*. For scholars of German this term, which was introduced into philosophy by Husserl, suggests a *world that is lived in*. Non-human animals are possessed of no such thing but there is a *world that surrounds them*, their *Umwelt*. A Lebenswelt is the product of what is often termed the "**matrix of categorization**" provided by a human language in that it determines what things can be experienced.

Time

11. The subjectivity of the experience of passing time is very well known; as Russell somewhere notes, with characteristic whimsy, five minutes spent sitting on a hot stove is rather more time than a whole hour in the company of a pretty girl. Those who have not learned to philosophize are afflicted by something they call "boredom" when nothing is happening around them, and then time does not pass at all. When something is happening what it is can be recounted in a narrative sequence. Time can be exploited as a model of itself as when a sequence of events is acted out by a mime-artist so that moments in time represent other moments. Indeed, Time is only brought into being through such representation. But it is the space provided by a material object—a sheet of paper or the wall of a cave—that must be adapted in making use of symbols. Exploiting once again our hieroglyphic model of language the semantics of a **narrative** can be seen to depend upon a model of Time that we should not be surprised to find in use in rudimentary form amongst our Neolithic forebears. This model is well known to readers of comic strips and consists of a linear succession of spaces to be filled by representations of what thereby become the episodes of a narrative.

For a narrative to be symbolized, what has to be acquired beyond the means of reducing a static picture to symbols is that of incorporating this organization of individual pictures into a string of symbols. In the case of the narrative depicted in the following sequence of pictures, the result might be something on these lines: 🏃 🐂 ▷ 🏃 ⚔ 🐂 ▷ 🐂 ⚔ 🏃. In this we see the ultimate semantics of such a narrative in natural language as "A man looked at a bison. Then the man chased the bison. Then the bison chased the man."

On cloudless nights we *see* the passage of time in the rotation of the stars about the pole and it is this motion that our mechanical clocks are ingeniously contrived to model. The circular clock-face divided into its hours and minutes is the representation of an interval of solar time and the boxes ticked off in turn in the matrix of the calendar that of longer intervals. More generally our picture of time is of motion along a regularly divided line. This is the semantics of "now" and "then."

Causation

12. There is much of the world that we cannot doubt we have in common with all human creatures. We cannot, for example, quite deny even the most primitive of people a certain insight into the impersonal *causality* of the world that dimly presages the achievement we call "Science." Such an insight can, however, seem to be dependent upon the peculiar representation of what is naturally present that is the use of language. I have used a hieroglyphic model of human language to suggest how the representation of events evolved from the primitive representation of things. Types of things emerged out of the *pictorial representation* of mere individuals and types of events in which they could be involved. But it is only the *symbolic reduction of pictorial representations* that can also allow types of sequences of events to emerge and impress themselves upon our minds. We have just seen how a syntactical innovation of a different order of abstraction would be called for to permit the writing of a formula on the lines of ♣ ▷ 🦑 to express the succession of one event, a flash of lightning, by another, a clap of thunder, in which a type of mark is employed which, in having

an exclusively syntactical function, is appropriately distinguished by us as a **symbol**. This hieroglyphic sentence serves as a model of such English sentences as, *"There was lightning and then there was thunder;"* in this way something that cannot be pictured in the way individual events can is represented and the human world has acquired an explicit temporal dimension.

The ability to make a symbolic reduction of such a succession also means that lightning, to continue our example, can now not only be followed by thunder but be followed by it on many different occasions: the two types of events can become constant companions in their fixed order in our symbolic representations: ✦ ▷ ✻ . . . ✦ ▷ ✻ . . . . And this must be the condition for the explicit recognition of a **causal nexus**, of a constraint, that is, upon what happens in the world of our experience. This recognition would only come with a further syntactical innovation introducing yet another symbol on the lines of this hieroglyphic sentence which is intended to model, *"When there is lightning, then there will be thunder:"* ✦ ▷▷ ✻. This gives expression to one aspect of the causality whose recognition is the condition of our being at home in the world in our more-than-animal way. Animals are driven by blind instinct or conditioned to behave in what seems only to us to be the same way when stimulated by what again seems only to us to be the same event.

Subjectivity

13. I suggested above that in addition to a fundamental *intuition* of causation each human being has an insight into the **motivation** of the others with whom he shares this world, with whom he competes and co-operates to exploit and husband its resources, and within whose society he pursues his career. The content of this insight is the representation he might make of a human creature. It would not do to represent such a creature in the manner of the bison-pictures on the wall of the cave, as a coloured outline, that is, having the shape of the animal. Such a device can only capture an *outer* appearance whilst our intuition of human being also comprises an *inner* being. It is only in virtue of this inwardness that we

understand the behaviour of our fellows, imputing to them as we do *beliefs* about the world they share with us and *intentions* to do something about it. In our un-philosophical moments we say that these are real mental occurrences hidden from us, but reflection will show that—like all other aspects of Reality—the inner life of another person is a feature of Modelled Reality that does not clearly subsist in any other way than in being represented by us. The model we linguistic creatures make is fashioned out of words: *"He thinks ...,"* we say, and *"he believes ...,"* and so, we conclude, *"he is going to... ."* But in terms of the hieroglyphic model of language introduced above the semantics of these phrases must involve a picture in which not just his outward appearance is shown (as in a picture of a tree or a bison) but also the inward goings-on. In understanding our fellows it is as though we also saw a picture of the world that only they can see and this inner picture must have its place in any adequate representation of a human being.

The series below represents situations which a speaker of English might describe with such sentences as *"There is a man and a bison,"* *"A man is* seeing *a bison,"* and *"A man is* imagining *a bison,"* respectively.

The syntactical resources with which we should have to provide our model language to reduce such pictures to symbols might result in formulæ along the lines of ⏍ 𝍫, ⏍ 𝍫 ⟦⏍⟧, and 𝍫 ⟦⏍⟧, respectively and here we have the fundamental semantics of all our linguistic ascriptions of their inner states to other people.

Hermeneutics

14. But something new arises with the advent of the inner pictures, for an artist does not suppose himself to *see* the inner contents of another human being in quite the same way that he sees that other's body. The latter presents itself *objectively*, as we say, and to make the contrast explicit we then also say that the former does so merely *subjectively*. What is objectively present might also be represented by another human being using the same symbols, so that in a situation where you and I were playing the favourite game of linguistically endowed human beings in exchanging observations upon our shared experience with one another, were I to write ⚑ 大 I should expect you to nod approvingly (for bison and men are no less present for you than they are for me), but should it seem to me that the man was thinking of shooting the animal and I were to write 大 【大 ⚑】, I should not be greatly surprised were you to insist upon, for example, 大 【🏠】, your interpretation of his inner goings-on beings at odds with mine in its seeming to you that he would rather just go home.

You may say that you know of the reality of the inner-life of others because you, being inside yourself, know of the reality of your own. But again, reflection will show that what you then have in mind is just another feature of Modelled Reality; indeed you apply to yourself the model that makes others intelligible to you. For what else could you do?—Nothing is anything to you until you have made a representation of it: you are nothing to yourself until you have your own self-representation! When a man intends his thinking to be rigorously objective, he only has to find a place for himself in his pictures for this goal to reveal its own illusoriness. If in such a picture he includes himself thinking about himself (as in the drawing above) then both the outer and the inner pictures are representations of one and the same thing. To express the recognition of himself as the maker of this picture he would have to make a second picture which showed the first as the inner picture associated with that same thing again. But since that thing is also the maker of the new picture a regress would be under way which could have no end. The picture that follows misleads for it shows several individuals rather than one and is not itself associated with any of them.

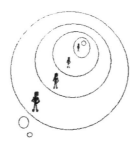

There could be no picture that showed a human being as both *present,* and as merely *represented* at one and the same time, so that here we can seem to arrive at the limits of what can be expressed. We have something that is no more substantial than the reflections within an empty hall of mirrors reflecting nothing but themselves. The drawing *refers to itself* in a situation—as we shall also have occasion to remark in the sequel—that is typical of the dissolution of meaning. We could, however, make this picture the semantic basis of a formula on the lines of ... 〖🏃〖🏃〖🏃〖🏃 ... 〗〗〗〗 ..., with the dots to indicate not just that it goes on and on but that it has no beginning as well as no end. However, the formula is no more meaningful than the picture from which it has been derived. We could go on to make use of a proper name in a formula like ... 〖🏃〖🏃〖🏃〖🏃 ... 〗〗〗〗 ... to indicate what no picture could alone, *viz.* that every token of the type 🏃 is a sign of one and the same individual thing. At this point syntax and semantics can seem to part company: what we express in language has transcended the natural meaning of pictures. But precisely because we cannot *picture* what the formula seems to say, we are still uncertain that we have grasped any meaning. Nothing is more transparent (and so impossible to see) than the ego that was supposed to be the clearly perceived starting point of the Cartesian philosophy. The interpretation of others that is demanded by our inability to *see* what might be going on inside them is the **hermeneutic** dimension of our human condition. A sophisticated psychology also has to recognize the hermeneutic dimension in our relationship to our own selves.

Weltanschauung

15. The notion of *Lebenswelt* already makes the objective observation of things and events in the world seem mere illusion in that nothing we experience exists quite independently of us. An analogy of this aspect of the human condition is provided by the printer's raster. The surface from which an impression is to be taken must be divided into imperceptibly small areas each of which in the process of printing will either be inked or remain clean. The image to be printed might be the artist's painting of a tree suggested in the diagram below. The diagram also suggests the image printed with a raster ruled in rectangles and with one ruled diagonally.

The first point of analogy is that just as in printed material there is no such thing as an un-rastered image, so in human life there is no such thing as an experience independent of some particular conceptual scheme. A second is that the rastering is something of which we are unaware until our attention is drawn to it. The rastering of a well-printed image makes no difference (for the screens are very finely ruled) to what we see and this is a point of disanalogy, for people who have adopted different conceptual schemes are not really talking about the same things.

But even to the extent our conceptualization is in agreement, what is experienced is different for different men. There are, indeed, differing global interpretations in which the things that exist for all men are given characteristic values that inform the behaviour of those who share them in particular ways. It is as though the rastering did make a difference—as though pictures printed with one screen showed things softly rounded whilst those printed with another gave the same things a jagged appearance. Each of these appearances would then be a **Weltanschauung**. This is another useful term of art in Philosophy; the literal meaning of the German word is *intuition of the world*, so that it might be rendered as *worldview*, but its dependence upon language can be recognized, as it often is, by talking of the "**discourse matrix**" of those who have adopted it. The particular *Weltanschauung* with which we are concerned in this essay is that of the scientist but its content is brought into relief by considering the unscientific alternatives. The matrix of conceptualization of the putative troglodytic users of our hieroglyphic model of language might well have its place for dragons—as, of course, does ours—for dragons can be as readily painted on the wall of a cave as bison, and paintings of them as readily schematized, for example in this form: 🐉. An encounter with a dragon is for us, no less than our ancestors, a possible experience, or, rather, it would be were it not that our *Weltanschauung* does not allow the reality of monsters. Nor, insofar as it is scientific and despite the places prepared for them in our matrix, does it allow the reality of ghosts or for a divinity that created the world or miraculously intervenes in the course of Nature. A *Weltanschauung* determines what phenomena there can be which means that only people who share one can experience one and the same world. People who use the same words can nevertheless only assert the same facts to the degree they share a *Weltanschauung*; insofar as they do not, they can neither agree nor disagree, for there is no common ground for their debate. We might both nod at being told that Drake's drum sounded at Trafalgar, but unless each also knows that the other is a man of the sort that believes in apparitions or that he is not but rather of the sort that has some appreciation of the mental disturbance of men in battle, then neither can know what the other's nod might mean.

Occultism

16. From what we know of the last remnants of Neolithic mankind surviving in jungles far away from our cities, we have little difficulty in imagining our ancestors confronted not by the *it* of our own transactions with inanimate things but by, in each case, another animate *thou* to be approached with the same circumspection as a human being. But primitive people seem also to believe themselves in possession of the capacity to control the world by manipulating not the things *present* in it but *representations* of them. This vicarious manipulation is the business of **magic** which, in those same jungles, apparently survives in such practices as harming an enemy by sticking pins in his effigy. It should be noted that this is no less *rational* a procedure than harming him by sticking pins in his living body (which is certainly one course of action an aggrieved scientist might consider). The witch-doctor conceives of the world in terms of similarities and analogies which in not being recognized by the scientist are **occult** conduits of causality. As we shall see the scientist too is guided in his thinking by similarity and analogy; however, he only recognize the reality of certain conduits including in particular the mechanical contact of material bodies. This difference separates two *Weltanschauungen*.

In our culture the *Weltanschauung* of occultism was elaborated in historical times in what—precisely because it was a rational exercise in the exploitation of analogy—might be designated the *proto-science* of Astrology. As is well known the astrologer carefully observes and records the condition of the heavens, by which is meant the instantaneous configuration of the wandering stars (the sun, the moon and the planets) against the background of fixed stars. This macrocosmic configuration is conceived of as a *representation* of the condition of the microcosm. That condition is the tendency of mundane events, of good harvests and plagues, that is, and of the fortunes of states, and princes and common men. This conception is rather sophisticated for it is one of *structure*, not of likeness. Its great virtue is that, on the basis of the periodicity found in the astrologer's records, the evolution of the heavenly configuration can be foretold with very great precision, so the evolution of events on earth can also be known in advance—at least to a certain extent, for there is with the astrologer a certain unscientific modesty: much of the occult relationship between the world of men and its representation in the stars is forever beyond our ken, it is something we cannot fully understand. For this reason the heavenly configuration is not read with certainty, but only *interpreted* with the wisdom of experience. The pronouncements of the astrologer always come with the proviso that he has made no error in his interpretation.

We do not count the work of the astrologer as scientific but it is instructive to make explicit our grounds for not doing so. There is at least the appearance of science in the characteristic product of the astrologer, *viz.* the horoscope. This is a highly developed device that might have had its primitive origins amongst troglodytes using our hieroglyphic model language. Looking up at the pattern of stars in the night sky they would have reduced it, as all primitive peoples seem to have done, to a degree of order by tracing in its chaos pictures of mundane things.

Their ability to do so would, of course, have been dependent upon the categorization established by their acquisition of language. The organization of a pattern would consist, in each case, in following the schema of one of the pictures that had become for them hieroglyphic words.

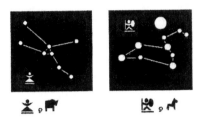

By tracing lines through the points of light in an area of the sky they might find here a bison, 🐂, perhaps, and there a lion, 🐕. The picture gallery in the sky would then have provided the background against which the course of wandering stars could have been plotted, the sun, schematically pictured on the lines of 🏹, in its moments of rising and setting before the brightest stars have quite faded, the moon, ☽, and others which are mere glowing points of light but for which hieroglyphic words would have supplied them with names to keep them from one another, 🧍 like our *Mars*, for example, or ⚖, like our *Venus*.

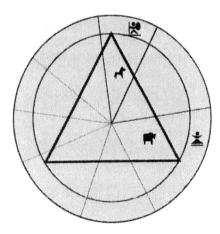

In this reduction to order of a keen observation of Nature there certainly is something of science and there is a good deal more in the determination of the fixed path through the constellations followed by the planets. The recognition that the points of the sun's rising on this ecliptic are correlated with the seasons of the year was vital, scientific, knowledge as soon as our ancestors left their caves to follow wild herds or sow and harvest grain.

The astrologer articulates the relationship between the celestial and mundane realms in the following elaborate manner. He makes what we call a *diagram, i.e.* a picture that has been reduced to geometrical elements. The diagram, known as a *horoscope*, consists of a circle with a circumferential annulus for the ecliptic and divided into segments for each of the star-pictures through which it passes. On this diagram—which is specific to a certain moment in time—each of the wandering stars has its instantaneous place. These places are marked with the astrological symbol representing the star (which for our hieroglyphic troglodytes could simply be its ordinary linguistic name) and the segments are similarly marked with appropriate symbols (which again presents no problem for our troglodytes). First the astrologer looks for geometrical relationships between the symbol tokens on his diagram by fitting the ends of diameters or the vertices of triangles or squares to his symbols. Thus Venus and Mars might be so aligned that he would find he could fit a triangle between ♁ and ♅ on his diagram. He would then combine each of these planetary symbols with those of the constellation in whose segment it is found, so that, continuing our conjectural example and assuming these to be ♍ and ♐, respectively, he might write ♁, ♍, and ♅, ♐. His diagram could now be reduced to a symbolic astrological formula which might be on the lines of ♁, ♍ △ ♅, ♐. There is nothing that strikes us as unscientific in any of this; quite the contrary, for we see something else that astrology shares with science: we see very clearly the *symbolic process* which can seem to be quite essential to the scientific mode of understanding. I have shown you the semantic basis of the astrological formula but I can find nothing more edifying to report about the use to which the astrologer now puts it than that he seems to allow his intuition, informed as it no doubt is by the wisdom of a lifetime, to crystallize, as it were, around it. *"The maiden in the house of the bison triangulates the warrior in the house of the lion,"* would translate the formula (which I do not suppose that any astrologer could find even remotely authentic) into English and we seem to grasp how certain poetic associations of the words involved could work in the occult imagination constructing something that could be presented as a plausible diagnosis of the condition of the cosmos and so of the tendency of events here below. The poetical exercise of the imagination is certainly not science; I would, however, be the last to deny that it may nevertheless be a very fine source of wisdom in the judgement of human affairs.

With all this show of science (and it is salutary to recall that not only did Newton have a profound interest in the ancient art but the last chair in Astrology at a prestigious European university was only vacated during the lifetime of Einstein) why do we not acknowledge it as such?—Well, its deficiency is not that the postulation of a relationship between heaven and earth is a false hypothesis, it is rather that this postulate is not a scientific hypothesis at all. But precisely why is that so?

Scientism

17. We have acknowledged that there is at least a little science in Astrology, and what little there is can be traced all the way back to the earliest human civilizations of Mesopotamia. It is for the historian of Science to offer an explanation for why there was not more. Such explanations are in terms of a lack of freedom to speculate in the great theocratic bureaucracies of the ancient world. What is thereby explained is how Science could emerge where, historically, it did. The oldest text of our Western civilization is the *Iliad*, Homer's burlesque satire upon whatever oppressive religion may have tried to hold its ground amongst the earliest Greeks. Its obese, effeminate coward of an heroic warrior, Achilles, is depicted listening to the sage counsel of his invisible mother, whilst her divine relatives occasionally take a rest from their own jealous quarrels to tip the balance with capricious disregard for anything that could be an ethical principle in favour of now one side, now the other in the great battle for Troy. Given the freedom to

which this testifies from the religious oppression felt by men in every other corner of the world, we have a satisfactory explanation for why the Greeks not only speculated about the nature of their world but also subjected their speculation to *rational criticism*, which again we recognize as an ineluctable condition of scientific thought.

But their nascent scientism has more than a tinge of the occult *Weltanschauung*. The ordered beauty of the heavenly circus is what above all impresses the astrologer and the fundamental notion of all Greek thinking is that of an eternal *cosmos*. There is nothing other than unvarying periodic change in this cosmos: what has to be understood is the irregular happenings in our world— in this sub-lunar sphere. In seeking to understand these the most systematic of Greek thinkers, Aristotle, whose ancient sobriquet is simply "The Philosopher," explicitly recognizes four different *principles of explanation*. It is particularly in such principles, whether or not articulated, that a *Weltanschauung* makes itself known. In Aristotle's intellectual world full understanding has been achieved only when each of these principles has been properly employed. The Aristotelian αἴτια (*aitia*) include the so-called *formal cause* which would accommodate the astrological nexus between the current configuration of the stars and the state of affairs on the earth below. We too might be able to grasp the heavens as a model of human society, but it is quite foreign to our way of thought to say that such a relationship could *explain* anything at all. And no less foreign is the principle that Aristotle himself finds most significant, *viz.* the τέλος (*telos*), the *final end*, that is, towards which the whole natural process is ultimately directed. In our scientific studies of the living world we find ourselves saying that, for example, the giraffe has an elongated neck in order to be able to get at the leaves other animals cannot reach, but we feel that such talk is merely provisional: one day we will explain why this is so in terms of a causation that involves *antecedent conditions* rather than *prospective outcomes*. Aristotle does indeed have a place for such explanations in his scheme (the *efficient cause* of things, as he would say) but for him the notion that events are explained as the effects of causes does not have the exclusive status it does in the scientific *Weltanschauung*.

The fourth of his *aitia* is the *material cause*; for us the notion that the sort of matter involved could be part of the explanation for a happening is also anathema: in our world, matter is something dead and everywhere the same. We recognize the notion of portions of matter imbued with special powers as characteristically occult, as we do that of special places in Space. That is, however, a co-ordinate part of the Aristotelian view of the world: each special type of sub-lunar matter has its own special place—for rock this is the centre of the earth, for fire the upper atmosphere, and so on—towards which it *naturally* moves whenever unconstrained. There is also *unnatural* movement—as when a rock is transported on a bullock-cart—but such perverse motion ceases as soon as does its cause. In the world of the moon and the sun and stars above, everything is already in its natural place and the only movement is that of going round in circles forever.

What we feel to be even more unscientific about the Greeks is their complete disinterest in **experiment**. There is a distinct Puritanism about the whole of their intellectual culture and as they contemplate Nature to discover the essence of things, it could not occur to them that there was anything to learn by interfering with her course. There is one achievement, however, that the historian is very inclined to claim for Science *viz.* the mathematical model of the heavens contained in Ptolemy's *Almagest*. But what this is a model of is, of course, the heavenly motions that are the empirical foundation of Astrology, so that it serves equally well a purpose conceived within either of our *Weltanschauungen*. It is, indeed, an ingenious and sophisticated elaboration of the annulus of the horoscope; if it is not the same *picture* as that painted by the Astrologer, then it is a picture drawn in the same perspective. And it is precisely the *perspective* that is unscientific.

Our scientific inheritance from the Greeks is a more critical use of rationality than the astrologer could permit himself together with a more sophisticated geometry than he had use for and it would be difficult to overestimate the importance of the ideal of intellectual freedom for the emergence of a new perspective. This freedom did not obtain in the Roman Empire and was channelled into theological hair-splitting in Christian Europe. But it had re-emerged when Leonardo was producing the drawings which testify to a passionate commitment to the close observation of Nature, on the one hand, and an unbridled delight in imagination, on the other. It is in the course of the Renaissance that the characteristic scientific conception of Man—if not the creator, then at least a re-creator of the world—is born. Man who until then has been satisfied to contemplate the handiwork of a creator conceives the Faustian ambition of uncovering the simple causes of Nature's process and by exploiting them making himself master of her forces. This is the new perspective and the first and still the most beautiful picture painted in it is the work of Newton—on the basis of the hesitant sketches of Copernicus, Kepler and Galileo.

The astrologer, and with him Ptolemy, paints his picture standing in his place here on earth and looking up at the stars. His is the picture of an artist anchored in his own world of passionate endeavour which, as we have seen, is precisely what he sees reflected back at him in the night sky. But Newton looks not up at the heavens wheeling about his own head but down upon the world with, as it were, the very Eye of God.

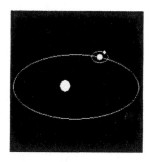

His first question is not, "What implication does this have for the accomplishment of my purposes," but rather "How is this done?" He sees nothing blasphemous in asking "How, given only sufficient power, could I do this?"—and therein lies the real significance of the familiar story of Newton's apple (which is repeated without too much attention to what is being said, as though to be aware that apples fall to the ground were an act of genius). I do not have before me whatever authentic details there may be, but the circumstances must have been somewhat as follows: there was not only a brilliant moon high in the sky but a fierce wind blowing as the greatest of human geniuses reclined beneath his tree and gusts of wind loosened the ripening apples from their branches, carrying them some distance from the tree. The strongest gusts would have carried an apple a considerable distance, perhaps over the garden wall, and Newton could have imagined a gust so strong that it gave an apple so much speed that it was carried into France before it reached the ground—or even right around the world and back into his garden, or even, why not, round and round the world for ever. For this is Newton's essential insight: that the speeding moon follows her orbit through the heavens in falling to earth just like an apple blown from its tree.

The forces at work in the world are natural ones; there are only those that make themselves felt as we go about our business. How could I make an earth to move about a sun and a moon to move about the earth?—I could do it, first, by coming to understand the blind forces that move apples or any other accretion of inert matter and then by arranging matter appropriately, for inert matter and mechanical force is all there is to the world. However, this is not to say that there is nothing occult, or hidden, or, in principle, beyond our understanding. For what is Gravity if not an occult force? Newton's own contemporaries were at first scandalized by the unscientific character of his theory, for the notion of the *action at a distance* of the earth upon the moon—or, for that matter, of the earth upon an apple hanging from a tree—can seem as occult as anything in astrology. Newton's reply to the challenge was to utter the famous words *Non fingo hypotheses,* by which he may have meant that he was not concerned with the sort of question that led the astrologer to conceive of the configuration of the heavens as a *sign* from a beneficent creator destined to help mankind in its struggle.

It goes without saying that we cannot have a theory of anything unless its subject has already been identified. In reviewing the familiar story above we have little trouble in deciding where the distinctive *Weltanschauung* of Scientism makes its presence felt. It is clearly present in the free speculation of the Greeks, in their submission to rational criticism, and in their quest for an underlying simplicity; there it is, again quite unmistakeably, in Ptolemy's mathematical model; and there in the close observation of Leonardo. For the man of Science, then, Nature—*it*, not *thou*—is an intelligible, rational realm of ordinary matter in a space which is everywhere the same and whose hidden mechanical causes, having first been discovered by sceptical, rational reflection upon the deliverances of his five senses, can, by the power of ingenious imagination, be bent to his own ends. The essential difference between the two *Weltanschauungen* we have considered is, on the one hand, the ultimate *thou*-ness of what is sought to be understood and, on the other, an original *it*-ness. A *thou*, but not an *it*, is an object of interpretation. It is as if someone were giving the astrologer a sign which he might or might not read correctly. What confronts Newton, however, is a piece of clockwork—a sign, perhaps, of a creator's mind at work—but he reads the face of the clock with no need to divine any hidden thought behind. To grasp more fully the scientific *Weltanschauung* we must study the peculiar way that the human power of reason is applied to this purpose. It is a lesson that we learned from the Greeks.

Summary

18. In this chapter the sense in which it is only in being *represented by us* that the world *is present to us* has been explained and the general consequence of this, that the reality with which Science is concerned can never be more than *modelled reality*, has been emphasized. Iconic models, especially *pictures*, have been identified as the foundation of all representation, and the relationship between *iconicity* and *language* explored with the help of a hieroglyphic model. The great importance of linguistic representation has been acknowledged and—because of its implications for our understanding of the nature of Science and, more

particularly, in anticipation of the theory to be presented in the sequel—special attention has been paid to the dependence of language upon the interplay of *syntax* and *semantics*. The particular importance of representation in language has been ascribed to the possibilities of *ampliation* which it alone allows. The way in which our use of language gives rise to a causally coherent *Lebenswelt* evolving through Time has been indicated and the notion of *Weltanschauung* introduced as a characteristic perspective upon the world in which we have our being. The pre-scientific (or, perhaps better, proto-scientific) conception of the world identified as *Occultism* has been discussed to provide a foil for the discussion of *Scientism* upon which we are now embarked.

INSIGHT

Geometry

19. There is a clear affinity between mathematical and scientific thinking. It will be necessary for our purposes to clarify how the two are related and a good place to start will be with a consideration of the earliest examples of mathematical thinking in which its essence is most easily seen. In such examples the form of representation rather than the matter represented is the object of enquiry. The subject matter of the first developed science, *viz.* Geometry, was the symmetry of points and curves. A drawing which consists of a single point has central symmetry (we can rotate the drawing about the point through any angle we please without changing anything) and the only curve that can be added to the drawing without breaking this symmetry is a **circle** with the point as its centre.

The only axes of symmetry of a drawing consisting of two points are lines that pass either through them both or else half-ways between them. The only curves that can preserve this symmetry are, then, the straight line on which they both lie and others that cross the first in such a way that all four of the angles between them are equal. Such equal angles are what we mean by "right angles."

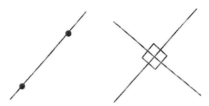

We seek symmetry in the artefacts we make and in the environment we build around us. We humans are undoubtedly very sensitive to the symmetry of points and lines (we admire objects possessing it, and it guides us as we construct our artefacts). The most primitive dwellings, constructed of leafy branches, have the *central* symmetry of circular huts, but in their building people who are still very primitive often prefer (as we moderns also usually do) the symmetry of *orthogonality*, that is: of three-dimensional structures based upon the right-angle. Now the men who built the pyramids were practical men who knew how to construct orthogonal edifices. They knew that if a line could be drawn across two others in such a way that the lengths of the intercepts were three, four and five, respectively, of the unit they used for measurement, the cubit, apparently, then two of these lines would be at right-angles to one another.

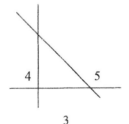

What we do not know is *how* they knew this, but they have left documents that plainly show they did. You *know* this and you know too, because it was hammered into you at school, that these numbers will work because the sum of the squares of three and four is the square of five. We see by imagining this drawing dilated that {6, 8, 10}, and so on, would also do as well as {3, 4, 5}, for we would in effect merely have doubled our unit of measurement. The Egyptians knew this too and may even have known other *Pythagorean triads*; it is not impossible that they even knew that, whatever number n might be, $\{(2n), (n^2-1), (n^2+1)\}$ is such a triad. They could certainly make magnificent (if oppressively un-modern) use of this knowledge, but they cannot have *understood* why they could use these numbers in this way and neither do they seem to have cared. Even in possessing the formula, and even in being able to derive it algebraically, there is no understanding of why the elements of Pythagorean triads *are* the sides of right-triangles. The interest of the Egyptians, like that of the Romans, was exclusively in getting things done; however, there were men in the ancient world who did care to ask why. Had the Greeks not done so (for they alone did care in the whole ancient history of humanity), then there might never have been men with a scientific *Weltanschauung* on this earth. In being moved by the desire for *insight* and not just for *getting it done*, they invented the means by which human beings come to the understanding which is within our reach.

Experiment

20. As we read the first real philosopher, Plato, we return to a point in time very close to the beginnings of the scientific enterprise. In the dialogue known as the "Meno" (because its dramatic setting is the house of an enlightened slave-owner of that name), Socrates seeks for the first time in human history an *understanding of understanding* (he conducts an "epistemological" inquiry, in the current jargon of Philosophy) by having a slave-boy who is quite untutored (this fact is of prime importance for Socrates—unlike in your case nothing had been hammered into his head in any school) discover for himself the first stages in arriving at the solution

of the mystery that did not interest the Egyptians or any other Barbarians (as the Greeks called them, and would have called us). Socrates draws a square in the sand and gently requires the boy to draw its *double* (by which he means one that has twice its area). Sand is not always a convenient medium in the situation in which a lecture is given or a book perused so I will pretend that he tore or cut a square out from a sheet of paper of the same sort as you might now have for hand.

The boy understands what is required of him and has, as we say, an *idea*. (It is interesting that we never know where our ideas come from: they are ultimately original mental events that simply happen to us.) His idea is that the sides of the doubled square are also doubled, *i.e.* that they will be twice as long as those of the original. He conducts the **experiment** that would confirm his hypothesis by making such a square. Now, you may feel no need to do this yourself because you can very easily *visualize* the result. It is, however, important that this is something that we can *do*. The doing required is so very simple that we can also do it in imagination but when things are only just a little more complex, we have to make at least a rough and ready drawing in the material world to be able properly to *see* (as we say in either case) what is going on. In carrying out his experiment the boy discovers that his original idea will not do: the new square is far too large. Indeed, he has only to fold it twice to see what we knew all along, *viz.* that doubling the sides does not double the original square but quadruples it.

Articulation

21. Now, why do I feel constrained to say that he *understands* that doubling its sides quadruples a square?—Well, what more could we ask of him than this? When he can make a square that has four times the area of Socrates' square in this manner and could clearly do the same with any square he might be given, what can possibly be said to be lacking in his understanding? And, conversely, how could he be said to understand were he unable to do this when presented with whatever square object it might be? A generalized capacity for doing seems to be not just the *sufficient* criterion for his understanding but also a *necessary* one. This is why we want to say that the Egyptian master-builders did not understand—for surely they did not. Socrates himself would not allow that the slave had understood until he had also *said* what it was he had understood: until, that is, he had articulated it linguistically and so given expression to it. Why does Socrates seem to be right in insisting upon this?—Is it because only articulate knowledge is *available* for use in other situations than that in which it emerged? Is it because understanding must be generally available in the form of a *law*? There is more to the problem than so, for the Egyptians certainly knew how an orthogonally symmetrical building was to be laid out, and they had their *law:* viz. *stretch out a rope 12 cubits long knotted together and with other knots 3 and 7 cubits from the first,* etc. We cannot pretend to have understood what Science is until we have answered this simple question.

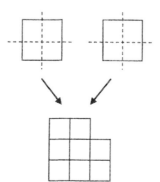

48

Exploration

22. In Plato's dialogue Socrates coaxes Meno's slave into seeing that as he has somehow to build a single square out of two squares of the same size as his original, he should start with two squares, not one, and explore their symmetry (although neither pupil nor master could have expressed what they were about in quite this way). Experiment shows that the bilateral symmetry about the axes that bisect opposite sides is of no help, because the eight small squares into which they suggest the originals might be divided cannot be arranged as a square. This is something you might not manage to *see* in your head and so find yourself making a rough drawing in the fashion of the one above. However, when the diagonal axes are considered, things are very different. This symmetry leads the slave-boy to divide each of his squares into two triangles (which we, if not he, can say are both "right-angled" and so lead our thoughts back to the pyramid builders) and he now has four more equal sides (where the squares have been dissected) that could become the sides of a single square.

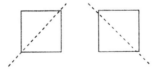

You may now feel the need to do more than just imagine the possibilities opened up by this dissection; you may feel that even a rough drawing is not enough to be able to *see* what is going on; you may feel the need to play with paper triangles a while, and not just contemplate them. What Meno's slave does is this: he manoeuvres the dissected squares alongside one another and then rotates the outermost triangles about their lowest vertices in this fashion.

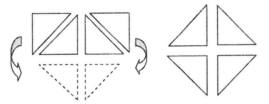

He has found—*by experiment*—how he can assemble these pieces as the doubled square that Socrates has been looking for, and with just a little prompting is even able to say that it is *the square whose side is the diagonal of the original*. He articulates, then, a more general empirical fact which he supposes with Socrates to be valid for any square that might be made out of paper, or drawn in the sand, or produced in any other way. He can seem then to regard his piece of paper as the concrete model of a reality that transcends merely material things. In this case the model is easily mistaken for part of this reality and the actors in Plato's dialogue must seem to use the words *line, triangle, square*, and so on, to name immaterial abstractions.

Necessity

23. We see that what the slave did with his cut and divided squares of paper in my not entirely faithful version of Plato's story we could also have done with any square object, of any size. His intuition has been educated (as has ours) and from now on he (as well as we) will see a square—any square—in a new light, for what we have learnt applies to all. You see why I urged you to do this yourself: it is *the mere doing* that educated us (if we did not know it before) as it taught him, first, that *the square on the doubled side of a square is four times the original*, and, secondly, that *the square on the diagonal is twice the original*. Socrates, however, prefers to say that it is as if these geometrical facts were items we remembered (not, of course, in the sense of a dim recollection of something to which we should have paid more attention in school, for the slave is supposed to have been quite untutored). But why *remembered?* It is as if what he has now learnt were something he had already known, for he could not doubt it in the way we can always doubt what our senses seem to show us (that a distant tower really is square and not round, for example, or that the stem of a reed growing out of a pond is bent at the surface). What the slave-boy has come to understand has a certainty that cannot be disputed: not only is *the square on the diagonal twice the original square,* but we want to say that it could not fail to be so: it is **necessarily**

so. Plato has a theory that is ridiculous to our modern sensibility concerning eternal souls that have once understood everything that we can come to understand but somehow forgotten most of it in the trauma of rebirth so that a fresh reminder must be given for such knowledge to be recovered. We prefer to say that what is manifest in the slave's achievement is rather the structure of human intuition. The slave—presumably a Barbarian, and not a Greek—discovers something about how he, as the rational human being he also is, cannot but think. He sees as a human being given the opportunity to play as he has been encouraged to do cannot but see.

Model Types

24. Something we could now do with the square we have constructed would be to fold each constituent triangle out over its own hypotenuse as shown in the next diagram. We could then, of course, fold the same triangles back into place again (as suggested in the series of diagrams below) and having seen all this, we can now go back to the 3-4-5 triangle of the pyramid-builders.

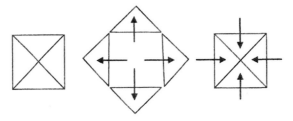

Is the reason why it is a right-triangle also something we can come to understand by similar means? Could we make right triangles by dividing rectangles that were not square along their diagonals and then fold four of them over to make a square in the same way? To arrive at an answer I think, you will find you absolutely must *do* the arranging and folding for yourself, because even this has a complexity that puts it beyond what we can imagine whilst being *sure* of what we really see. What happens is not quite the same as when we began with a square, for we discover that there is a hole in the middle that could be filled by a little piece of paper which we easily see would be a square the length of whose side was *the difference between the long and the short sides* of the rectangle.

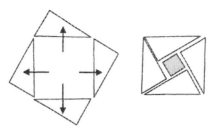

We would, however, grasp a similarity between the two cases in recognizing that the drawings are the same except that in the case of the slave's the side of the square is of zero length. And this symmetry can be exploited in doing with this square—with these five pieces of paper which together add up in area to *the square on the diagonal*—what the slave did with his: we have done it before, so we can do it again: we can re-arrange them by moving two triangles so that they form complete rectangles with the other two. Having done this we would immediately see that their combined area *is equal to the sum of the squares on the sides* of the triangle because the line I have indicated in the diagram divides a square equal to that on the smaller side (to its left) from one equal to that on the larger. (This line is an axis of dilated bilateral symmetry, for whilst there is a square on either side, they are of different sizes.)

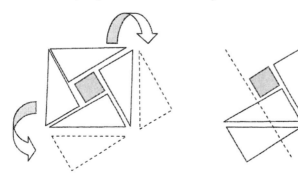

We began with a rectangle and divided it in two along the diagonal. We did not exploit anything *special* about this triangle, so that it might as well have been just any right-angled triangular object, made of paper or anything else convenient. We could then have begun with any other, copied it to make a rectangular object and then proceeded exactly as before. The triangle would be a *model* (one of endlessly many material models we might have made). There is a sense, then, in which this model is just one *token* of a *type* of model. Producing the ensemble of four triangles and a square is something that we could have done with any token of the type; it is in this sense that the result we have arrived at is *an invariant of the model type.*

Certainty

25. In recognizing this invariance we have understood the mystery about which the Egyptians did not find it necessary to puzzle their heads, for one of the tokens of our model type is a rope stretched out as a triangle two of whose sides are of three and four units of measurement, respectively. Variations of our drawing are found not only in Greece but also in Babylon (where it may have originated), in India, and in China. But only in Greece was this not enough, for there amongst the fathers of Science a doubt remained. What seems to be so can often show itself to be quite otherwise. *How, then, can we be certain that the triangles and the little square really fit together as they seem to do?* Ours certainly do not, for we cannot draw, tear or cut lines which are as straight as we might like them to be—as they *ideally* ought to be in a demonstration such as this. We need some assurance that is independent of the grossness of matter, the crudeness of our tools, and the limits of our skill. It is this deficiency that Euclid sets himself to provide. His starting point might have been the problem that Socrates set for Meno's famous slave. Here is a drawing of the squares on the three sides of an equilateral right triangle (the triangle produced by dividing a square along its diameter).

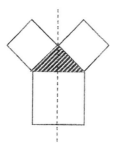

We are human beings as Euclid was and similarly sensitive to symmetry and asymmetry; we are struck as we consider it (or at least as soon as it is pointed out) and as Euclid must also have been by its bilateral symmetry about the axis shown in my drawing, in which the triangle's right-angle is now at the top (this is the drawing celebrated as *The Windmill*). We seem to know (for this was the conjectural stating point) that the square on the diagonal has twice the area of that on either side, and we see *by symmetry* that this axis divides the square on the diagonal in two, so we also seem to know that each half has the area of the square on a side. We can, of course, be mistaken in taking an object for symmetrical, but there can be no arguing with *the insight that comes with the perception of symmetry:* in so far as this is an axis of symmetry, there is no question that the squares and half-squares are equal. Symmetry is of itself a warrant at least as authoritative as the conclusion of any exercise in logic.

But might we not still be mistaken?—Might this not merely seem to be an axis of symmetry? We become mathematical thinkers when we find ourselves drawn to *proving* that it really is. To that end we shall have to *do* a couple of other things first (our proof will require a couple of *lemmas*, as a mathematician would say). If we make a paper square (or, more generally, a rectangle) and then tear off a right-triangle from one side and move it over to the other, then the result is a parallelogram of the same height as the original square. We have not thrown any paper away so it must also be of the same size as the original square.

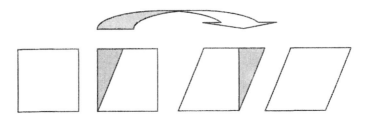

Having done this, we recognize the invariant of a model type and understand that all parallelograms on the same base and between the same parallel lines have the same area as the rectangle of the same height on that same base; this is our first lemma. (In the edifying way of lecturers pressed for time, I "leave it as an exercise" to elaborate the game being played here to extend this result to cases in which the apex of the triangle falls beyond the further side of the square—which is the case which we will actually need to apply.) The other thing we have to do is to consider a paper parallelogram and recognize the symmetry along the diagonal.

More precisely, what we see is that by turning one of the triangles over we could place it on top of the other. We know by this symmetry that the triangles divided by this axis are equal to one another. Consideration of the invariants of the model type shows us that *any parallelogram—including, then, any square—has twice the area of any triangle of the same height and on the same base*; this is our second lemma.

Returning now to the Windmill-drawing, we readily find opportunities for exploiting all that we have now *understood by doing*. We can begin with the triangle and square marked below in this pair of copies of the original: the triangle is half the square. You know this when you do again in imagination what we did above—or, more to the point, what I left you to do as an exercise—as you tore off triangles and moved them to the other ends of squares before folding the resultant parallelograms in two along their diagonal. It is in such imaginative doing that **insight** consists! Understanding is having insight—it is *being able to imagine what will happen when something is done.*

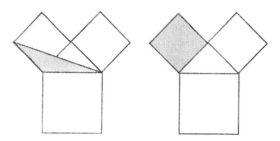

What is true of the triangle and square above is no less true of the triangle and the half-square rectangle marked in the next pair of drawings.

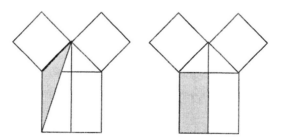

But we also see that there is more symmetry here—this time rotational, for we could rotate either of the triangles we have marked about their common vertex to exactly cover the other. We are now certain that the square and the half-square rectangle above are equal in size. But by symmetry we are certain of something more, we know that the half-square is precisely that, so we also know that the whole square on the diagonal is—as Meno's slave-boy was able to recall for Socrates—twice the original square. (However, if you did not do what I left as an exercise you are, perhaps, still not sure of anything—which was, of course, what I intended to demonstrate.)

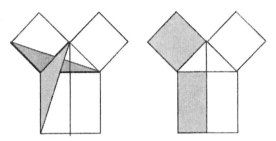

Bedrock

26. As we have said, the point of going to all this bother—this quasi-Euclidean exercise—when what the slave did to arrive at the same result was so much simpler is to make *certain* that what *seemed* to Socrates, to Meno, to the slave, and to us to be so *really* was. We should now be certain were it not that we have relied upon the lemmas concerning rectangles, triangles and parallelograms. Euclid is, however, able to show us that we need be no less certain about these. Our doubts (including one about whether the triangle we rotated really was congruent with the other) are pushed further back—right back to what Euclid himself is satisfied is *bedrock*, right back to what can no more be doubted than symmetry itself, right back, that is, to what seem to be indubitable principles of reasoning. Euclid lists these for us at the beginning of his *Elements*; here they are together with diagrams that would have assured him, as they do us, that he is not deceived.

Whole figures that will cover one another are the same:

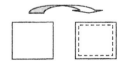

A whole is greater than any of its parts:

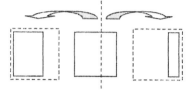

Two wholes each the same as a third are the same as one another:

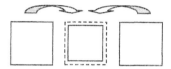

If the same part is taken from the same wholes, then the remainders are the same:

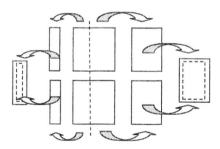

The intended sense of "the same" is, in each case, "of the same size" and Euclid also relies upon the similar recognition that *If the same wholes are added to the same wholes, then the new wholes are the same.* In our exposition above we made use of much of this insight into the nature of wholes and their parts without even noticing and it is quite naturally the case that what cannot be doubted has this unremarkable air of stultifying triviality whenever it is explicitly enunciated.

Having done all this Euclid could now consider the more general case of the triangle produced by dividing a rectangle that is not a square. The result he wants is achieved immediately *by symmetry*; not, however, the *bilateral* symmetry of the

Windmill-drawing of the squares around an equilateral right-triangle, but the *structural* symmetry of the diagram below in which what is to the right of the axis has been dilated. For either symmetrical half, the reasoning presented above is an indubitable demonstration that the complementary rectangular parts of the square on the diagonal is equal to the square on the corresponding side.

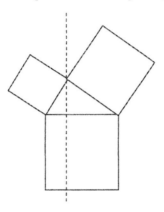

Genius

27. But having gone to all this trouble we will now have to admit that what Pythagoras claims to teach us as a great novelty (and he is said to have been so pleased with himself on discovering his proof that he sacrificed a hundred oxen to his gods) was, in fact, quite *obvious* all along—at any rate to an intuition which has been educated by sufficient experience of dilative symmetry. When a geometrical figure is dilated the result is a larger figure that is *similar* to the original in that the angles between its lines are the same and their lengths are in the same proportions to one another. This entails that the figures fill the same proportions of the areas of the rectangles with which they might be circumscribed.

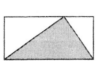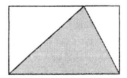

In the same way similar rectangles will each occupy the same proportion of squares erected on their corresponding sides.

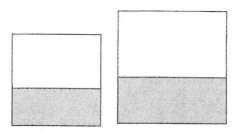

But this insight is already all one needs to see that what Pythagoras has to say about right-angled triangles is just as he says it is. Consider the drawing below: any right-angled triangle, (i), can be divided into two by dropping a perpendicular onto its hypotenuse from the right-angled vertex. The two new triangles, (ii), are then not only right-angled but also similar to one another and to the original triangle—as we can see by imagining them stacked on top of one another, (iii). The three similar triangles can be folded out to stand on the three sides of the original, (iv). The areas of the two smaller triangles are equal to that of the third, *i.e. the triangle on the hypotenuse is equal to the sum of the triangles on the other two sides*, so that, given our observations above concerning similar figures, Pythagoras' result is now, as I said, *quite obvious*. Once we have seen this, and I am inclined to say only upon that condition, we have understood the Pythagorean Theorem; in an intuition that is sufficiently educated we *see* that things could not be otherwise. What we mean by "insight" is the recognition of such obviousness, and that is precisely what constitutes understanding. If there be any such thing as mathematical genius then it is presumably the ability to see what is *obvious* in an unelaborated drawing of a geometrical figure without the pedestrian preparation through which you have just been led.

60

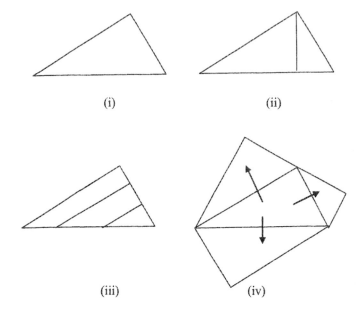

(i)   (ii)

(iii)   (iv)

Summary

28. This chapter has been a sustained discussion of the famous geometrical theorem of Pythagoras. Its theme is the contrast of the *practical* knowledge of the Egyptian pyramid-builders with the *theoretical* knowledge of the Greek mathematician. The part of *experiment* in attaining such knowledge was emphasized and the exploration of *symmetry* identified as its particular form in at least the case of Geometry. The general goal of articulating a *law* was pointed out and the *necessity* that characterizes such laws ascribed, in Kantian fashion, to the structure of the *human mind*. More particularly the rôle played by model-building was carefully considered and the crucial notion that a law is an *invariant* of some *type* of models was canvassed. The practical competence and theoretical ignorance of the Egyptians was accordingly ascribed to their possession of nothing more than individual *tokens* of the Pythagorean type. The process of reasoning that led to the theoretical knowledge of the Greek geometers was

somewhat speculatively reconstructed in sufficient detail to demonstrate its dependence upon the manipulation of a physical model. The trivial principles exploited in reasoning about these manipulations were made explicit in order to emphasize their indispensability. Finally, the notion of *insight*, which will be of great importance below, was introduced by identifying a stroke of mathematical *genius*—*i.e.* the unmediated apprehension of theoretical knowledge—with its unprepared visitation.

REASON

Warranty

29. The style of thinking that we call "mathematical" was demonstrated above. It consists in seeking not just insight into the way things are but *warranted* insight. There is no doubt that unwarranted reliance upon insight is as foreign to the scientist as it is to the mathematician so that this is the basis of the relationship between their enterprises. But we have still barely touched upon how mathematical insight is warranted. For a proper understanding of this it is important to recognize that the numerals—which, alongside geometrical drawings are of particular importance in mathematical thinking—are also (unlike drawings) *words*, and a consideration of how they get their meanings will emphasize the essential rôle of the special form of doing we call *games-playing* in our ampliative use of language and so in our science. We can easily imagine a game, the Counting-Game, that a human creature with a rudimentary language might play. These are its rules: the player surveys the things with which he intends to play (perhaps *trees, or bison,* or just plain *things* for which he has names) and then points at them in turn. To do this he must, of course, have some language because, as we have seen, things would not otherwise be categorized for him, so that he would not be able to point at a bison rather than a herd, a horn, a wound, a hoof-

print or a shadow. As he points at each of the things he is interested in, he cuts a notch with his honed flint in a convenient stick. When he is done he makes a memorandum by making somewhere a picture of the pattern of marks on the stick. He would only have to do this stereotypically for his drawings to be apt for assimilation to the existing words of our model hieroglyphic language as the numerals corresponding to "one," "two," and so on.

◆ ◆◆ ◆◆◆ ◆◆◆◆ ◆◆◆◆◆

The syntax of the language would have to evolve to accommodate them, perhaps so as to make, for example, the sequence ◆ ◆🐾 ⚔ ◆◆◆ 🧍 the title of a picture in which three men were being chased by two bison. Clearly, given only a sufficiently long stick, the game of counting need never give out and neither need a hieroglyphic vocabulary of numerals: just as is the case for our language, whenever our troglodyte had a type of mark to serve for any numeral, he would also be able to institute the use of one to serve for the next.

Number

30. The first mathematicians—who were also the first philosophers—played with collections of pebbles on the beaches of Sicily and what is now Turkey. The game they played, this game of *counting*, is one we humans invented in something like the manner just suggested, but the remarkable thing about this invention of ours is that denumerated collections of categorized things have properties that we neither intended nor foresaw and which therefore seem to be in some sense independent of us and our game-playing. As in the case of many other words we suppose the numerals to be the names of certain things, *viz. numbers*, things we have *discovered*, not *invented*. The earliest Greek mathematicians made no distinction in their thinking between these numbers and collections of pebbles, but in whatever sense it may be that numbers are real items, they are not palpable entities, no more so than are the squares and triangles with which geometry is concerned, so that we are inclined to designate them *abstractions*. A particular collection of pebbles on the beach, on the other hand, is something *concrete*, a

concrete model of the abstract number. It is a model not in the sense of bearing a perceptual resemblance to the number—for nothing could resemble an abstraction (which is a large part of what it means for something to be "abstract")—but in being entities with which we can do what we also do with numbers: it is a *functional* or *operational model* rather than an iconic one. Our numerals are names for the real things and allow us to model them in our language. A collection of pebbles is a plastic model of a number; in playing games with such collections it is as though we were playing with the real things—the numbers— themselves, which in their apparent independence from us seem to be more than mere artefacts of our representation. It was in this *vicarious play* with Reality that rigorous mathematical thinking historically began.

The fundamental game that can be played with these model numbers is one of *arrangement*, and the fundamental arrangement of groups of pebbles is to string them out in rows to make linear patterns just like those on a tally. Pebbles can be arranged not only in lines, however, but also in other plane geometrical figures including, of course, the triangles, squares, pentagons, and so on, of Geometry.

Whereas Geometry is the study of continuous structures, such as Pythagoras' triangles, Arithmetic is that of discrete ones, such as collections of pebbles. The Greeks do seem to have conceived of Mathematics as a unified whole but the geometrical arrangement of discrete elements turns out not to be the way to effect the unification. The first mathematicians were particularly interested in arrangements of pebbles in rectangles. This is a game that any human child will quickly catch on to, but no picture could show *naturally* what is required. For that a diagram is needed which relies upon some *convention*. The particular convention which is so universally applied in our culture that it can seem to be natural makes use of dots to show what a player has to do in some indefinite situation and thereby in any situation whatsoever.

We would not be surprised to see a child at play doing this, but what comes next is more surprising. When we make such a rectangle we are (as we say in our developed mathematical jargon) *multiplying* the number of pebbles laid out as a base by the number of rows laid out above it, but when we do this in reverse and starting from a model number try to see what rectangular arrangements we can make of the collection of pebbles, then we are, as we say, *factorizing* the number itself, and it is in such factorization that we first come into contact with a reality independent of our volition, for we quickly discover that certain collections cannot be arranged in this way. Some numbers are *different* from the run of the mill and this difference of theirs is exactly what seems to demand an explanation. The different ones, those greater than 1 that cannot be factorized, *i.e.* 2, 3, 5, 7, and so on, are the *prime numbers*. They summon the attention of the mathematically inclined because they are the *ultimate factors* of all other numbers in this sense: any collection of pebbles that is not the model of a prime number can be arranged as a rectangle with a prime number as its base, as suggested in the diagram below. Starting from any such collection we are able to do the same (using the same or a different prime number) with any one of the columns of the rectangle we have made, and go on doing so until we are left with a prime number of pebbles on both side of the rectangle and so come to a stop.

Thus a collection of 12 pebbles is arranged in this way into a 2 x 6 rectangle, and then one of its columns as a 2 x 3 rectangle. Both 3 and 2 are linear numbers, so that we have decomposed 12 into its ultimate factors 2, 2 again, and 3: all prime numbers. We see then that our invention of the counting-game has brought into being—*without our having intended anything of the sort*—a set of ineluctably linear numbers out of which all others can be composed as rectangular ones.

This game with pebbles is childishly simple, but the recognition of prime numbers is in fact—and that right at the beginning of Man's scientific career—a confrontation with one of the very greatest of intellectual mysteries: we simply do not know what it means. When you go for a walk in the mountains, the track you follow leads you hither and thither, and up and down. The track exists independently of you, and would be there had you never set out upon it. Indeed the landscape would still have been there had nobody ever trod that way. It can seem to be the same with numbers: they seem to exist just as independently of us. It is as though they were features of a reality that transcends our being and our powers of imagination, a reality which is modelled by our game with pebbles (our calculus, as we say, "calculus" being the Latin name for a little stone). But now consider the game of *Chess*: it too has consequences which its inventors cannot have intended, but which players discover as the "theorems" of the game (for example, that a certain ensemble of pieces—just two knights accompanying their king, for example—either can or cannot mate the lone enemy king). Which are we to say—that *Chess* too is part of a transcendent Reality, or that *Arithmetic* is nothing more than an artefact of our play? The question becomes important when we try to grasp what Science is *about*. The scientist appropriates the mathematician's style of thinking and hurries on his way; the philosopher, albeit wistfully, can choose to put the mystery aside and follow after to see where these modern sages will lead. We shall see how they are guided in the same way by their play with the models they make.

Hypothesis

31. With the remarkable discovery of prime numbers the unintended features of the game we have invented are only beginning to unfold. It was in deliberately seeking them out and recording them that the Greeks started humanity on the path to *Science*. For example, it might at first seem that there are only a few of these recalcitrant linear numbers, but the first scientific thinkers set about looking for more and quickly found 11, 13, 17, 19, 23, and so on, on and on. Just as we can go on counting without end, there seemed to be no end to the sequence of primes. Now an **hypothesis** is a supposition (the Greek word means something like *foundation*: it is something *put down* upon which an argument is subsequently built but it is only a provisional foundation because it will be rejected if the argument fails); it is a guess, but not an idle one—an interesting and worthwhile hypothesis is rather a supposition that there is some good reason to entertain. The good reason, in this case as in many others, is a series of experimental observations: we try the *experiment* of making a rectangle with 29 pebbles and find that we cannot succeed (we know, indeed, that we will never succeed because there are only nine prime numbers that could be the base of the rectangle, so we can quickly try them all); it is then an experimental *fact* that 29 is a prime number. On the basis of the seeming endlessness of the series of primes, the first mathematicians formulated the hypothesis that *there is no greatest prime number*. But they did not stop with the mere hypothesis; they went on to confirm it, that is, to prove to their own satisfaction that this hypothesis is true in the precise sense that it mirrors the Reality to which the numbers belong. Here we see already the fundamental pattern of "scientific" investigation.

Confirmation

32. And how did they confirm their hypothesis?—Well, said Euclid (who is conventionally given the credit for the important mathematical discoveries of the earliest Greeks) simply imagine that you have found the greatest prime (it is of no

little importance that you must *imagine* this). Now imagine yourself making a linear number by multiplying together all the primes. Next add 1 to the collection. To imagine this you will, of course, have to take a specific example (it would surely be self-delusion to suppose that what you were imagining was just any prime number). Suppose that 5 were the last prime number, so that there would be no others than 2, 3 and 5. What Euclid requires of you is that you multiply 2, 3 and 5 together to make 30. What you next have to do is to add one more pebble to the collection which models this number. Having done so you see that you cannot arrange the new collection as a rectangle because whether you try with 2, 3 or 5 as base, there is always one troublesome pebble left over. What you have imagined, then, is a prime number, 31, that is greater than 5, the hypothetical greatest prime with which we began. However, what we have imagined ourselves doing with 5, we could also imagine ourselves doing with any other prime number, including in particular any which we took to be the greatest of them all. We see, then, that, despite what we supposed, we cannot after all imagine a greatest prime.

I have now shown you the piece of reasoning that confirms that there is no greatest prime number. What will be important in the sequel is that the process of reasoning, albeit more or less effortless, is quite opaque: we did it easily but without *seeing* what we were about. The drawing above is an attempt to suggest what we might have been imagining as we went along by exploiting the conventional device of rows of dots introduced above. Just as we say "a bison is chasing a man" without seeing how we mean anything by it, we do not see what reasoning is until we have made a model for ourselves, in the former case the hieroglyphic language introduced earlier, and in the latter a drawing like this.

Critique

33. Compare these two discoveries (that there are prime numbers, and that there is no greatest amongst them). The first we can suppose was made in a pedestrian way by trial-and-error: all the possibilities of arrangement with a prime number already discovered as the base of a rectangle having been tried without success, a number was declared to be "prime." But the second is far more impressive. Since there is clearly no end to the game of making numbers, trial-and-error cannot even be contemplated. In making such a general statement as "there is no greatest prime," we are using language to criticize the pictures we seem to be able to make (in this case one that would show the greatest prime). We find that we cannot *consistently* imagine any such thing—a number, that is, with which one could not perform this operation of multiplication and addition; it is a truth of the reality to which these abstract things we call numbers belong that there is no such thing. What seems to be happening here is that reason discovers a constraint upon our imagination which, in its turn, imposes a constraint upon our possible experience with collections of pebbles. Insofar as this piece of mathematics can be taken as a paradigm of scientific thinking, what that consists in is *the critical consideration of what ideally rational creatures can and cannot imagine themselves doing with their models of Reality.* We understand a particular feature of our experience when we have grasped why it has to be as it is. And this we have done once we have satisfied ourselves that *we cannot imagine it being otherwise.* Because we can often be unsure whether we have consistently imagined what we suppose ourselves to have imagined, conviction may only be obtained by *real doing* with some model of the matter in question. It was by successfully arranging your collection of thirty pebbles as rectangles with various bases and failing to do the

same when one more was added to the collection that you arrived at the insight we have been discussing, and it was in seeing that it could make no difference whatever base you tried—in that each failed trial was a *token* of one and the same the same *type of failure*—that this insight was confirmed.

Coherence

34. The drawing above shows this type and having been generalized by the convention of dots. it was intended to apply not just to 31 but to any number similarly related to all primes less than itself. But this intention had to be explained, for whilst a picture can show us something, only a sentence can make a point about what is being shown. It is only language that makes it possible to reason about what we have seen. I have insisted upon the *opacity* of our sentences in the sense that we cannot immediately see how they implicate one another as constituents of a piece of reasoning any more than we could immediately see how individual words come to have the meanings they do. Reasoning is something we do with language with as little explicit awareness of how we are doing it as when we describe the scene before us or our own feelings. A point concerning a picture or model could only be made in a text, but no explanation has so far been offered of our capacity for putting individual sentences together to compose such a text coherently. (A text, as I shall use the word, might be oral rather than written: it is any complex symbolic structure; mathematicians are particularly concerned with the texts they call "proofs" and scientists with those they call "*theories*.") To understand the provenance of **coherence** we have to imagine our ancestors playing not *language-making games* (like those we played earlier with hieroglyphs) but *language-games*—games played with language rather than in making it (like the game of tallying considered above), the games a language-user can play but not a mere picture-maker. In particular we must consider the games whose object is the coherent *ampliation* of a text, that is to say: the drawing from it of more than is said in it.

Analogy

35. It is as material for analogical reasoning that models have their place in Mathematics. Recalling that things only exist at all in being represented by us, the most primitive use of such reasoning must have been in the comparison of representations, in saying, that is, how things were the *same* as one another and how they *differed*.

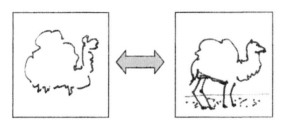

Things can be the same or different in appearance, *e.g.* a certain cloud on the horizon might be like a camel. In our model language the expression of this *simile* would require a syntactical innovation, and something like this might serve: 🐫 88 🐫₀ The new symbol is not iconic, for there is nothing we see for it to resemble; the category it brings into being is not a type of things but one of relations amongst pictures: its semantic basis is, then, something that it invites us to *do* with pictures. More interestingly for the scientific thinker different things can be *counterparts* of one another in having the same structure or function, thus, *e.g.*, there is a sense in which its shell is to the turtle what his house is to a man. There is hardly anything of scientific interest to be drawn out of this particular analogy, but other cases suggest how analogy is in fact the basis of all scientific thinking, thus what impressed Newton, for example, was the sense in which the motion of the moon around the earth is *like* that of a conker whirled on a string, and what impressed Darwin, was the sense in which the fate of an animal within its natural environment is *like* the selection of a ram by a farmer breeding sheep.

Nothing more can be done with what is still mere metaphor until further syntactical innovation allows the composition of a sentence as the expression of the specific co-ordination of terms that constitutes the analogy. The game in which this was explicitly expressed might take the form illustrated in this diagram.

In the model of language to which we have had recourse the recognition that the relationship of its carapace to a turtle is *just like* that of his house to a man might be manifest in writing a sentence on these lines: 🐢 8 🏠 88 🏠 8 🧍₀ The most significant metaphorical identification of this kind is that of mentality and sensory perception: having an idea is *like* seeing some material thing. Now, it is human to recognize that *you are the same as me* in particular in that you too have an inner-life that is directly accessible only to you: a mind, that is, of your own. This recognition may be instinctive (as all small children—other than those unfortunates who are autistic—do quickly attain it); if, however, we seek to reconstruct it as a piece of reasoning then it becomes the earliest and the most important use of analogical reasoning. The first part seems to be on these lines: *thinking is like sensation, so that we perceive our ideas just as we do the things about us. Things are seen and so too are ideas.* The process of thought involved is clear when this is expressed in the following pedantic fashion:

Thought is like sensation;
i.e. *the subject is related to his ideas just as the subject is related to things*
The relationship between subject and things is that of seeing.
So the relationship between subject and ideas is that of seeing.

A *symbolic model* of this piece of reasoning can be approached by borrowing syntactical symbols from our hieroglyphic model—as is not inappropriate since in constructing that model I borrowed them from mathematical practice in the first place.

Thought :: *Sensation*
subject : ideas :: subject : things
(subject : things) = seeing
_____
(subject : ideas) = seeing

This is, then, a symbolic model of the hidden process that leads to the notion that thinking is seeing ideas; it consists of the representations of four different sentences, the *premisses* of a particular analogical argument, which are separated by a ruled line from the final sentence which is its *conclusion*. We arrive at a symbolic model of this piece of reasoning that makes it one *token* of a *type* of reasoning processes in the following manner: we allow A and B to be the words giving expression to the analogy for the two things being compared (*viz. thought* and *sensation*, respectively) and, similarly, a_1 *(subject)* and a_2 *(ideas)* and b_1 *(subject* again) and b_2 *(things)* to be the parts of these things identified with one another as the basis of the comparison. Then, using, finally, C to represent the relationship named by *seeing*, we can represent what we seem to be saying to ourselves in this manner:

$A :: B$
$a_1 : a_2 :: b_1 : b_2$
$(b_1 : b_2) = C$
_____
$(a_1 : a_2) = C$

The model is hardly adequate, for a problem that has to be acknowledged with all analogical reasoning is that the two things compared are always *like* one another—in scientific cases usually in that they work like one another—but without being the *same*. Inevitably, then, there will be points of **disanalogy** as well as of *analogy* and these must not be allowed to lead to any conclusion. Thus an adequate model would have to represent the more sophisticated reflection that disallowed certain conclusions. It might then seem to us properly to reflect our reasoning not just in the case of thought and sensation but also in many others (those involved in grasping my remarks above about Newton and Darwin, for example) and we should then be tempted to regard it as presenting what is essential to any example of analogical reasoning. In being accorded such a status it would have become the **canonical model** of all analogical reasoning: reasoning which could be represented by the model would be valid and analogical reasoning which could not would be tainted with irrationality. As philosophers we should then have to agonize over whether this validity had any other reality than that which the model conferred upon it. However, what we accept as analogical reasoning independently of any model seems to be—as the primary form of creative thinking that it is—too varied to be captured in any simple formula.

Induction

36. The conclusions we arrive at by analogical reasoning are modal: we do not, for example, conclude that ideas *are* things seen, but rather receive the suggestion that they *may be* so. An alternative process of reasoning is exemplified by an argument on these lines: *All the swans that have been observed were white. So all swans are white.* Such an argument is dignified with the title of *inductive generalization*. Nobody would offer precisely this argument in our days because it is a well-known ornithological fact that the swans of Western Australia are black. Consideration of this one very familiar example alone teaches us that before these swans had been observed this argument was unsound. One might have arrived at a sound argument on these lines: *All the swans that have been observed were white. Probably then, all swans are white.* One might even reasonably have ventured this: *Countless swans have been observed. No non-white swan has ever been*

observed. Very probably then, all swans are white. But the single historical fact of the *falsification* of the unqualified argument demonstrates not only its unsoundness but the general unsoundness of any argument of this type:

All the A's that have been observed were B's

All A's are B's.

Precisely because it is susceptible to **falsification**, the sound judgement that some generalization is *probably* correct is not of very much use to the scientist except, that is, in the generation of hypotheses to be warranted by a further exercise in reasoning. But things are very different with a falsified argument, because the conclusion arrived at by falsification is more than merely probable. Consider this premise: *A black swan has been observed.* Its immediate conclusion is not: *It is* probably *so that not all swans are white* but *It is* necessarily *so that not all swans are white.* This process of reasoning belongs neither to analogy nor to induction but to *deduction.* Despite a certain confusion that originates with venerable Aristotle, "necessarily" has no other meaning than "it follows as the conclusion of a sound argument."

Deduction

37. One language-game to be played with our hieroglyphic model is the keeping of a log of interesting events—of "empirical observations" in the parlance of Science. But as we noted earlier sequences of events are more worthy of attention than individual ones, so that the syntactical resources that allowed a note to be made of successive occasions upon which, in our example, lightning was followed by thunder, ♣ ▷ ❀, could prepare the way for the introduction of the symbol that will model the most important of all words in the mathematical and scientific vocabularies, the intermediate symbol in the following formula: ♣ ▷▷ ❀. What the formulæ it models are intended to convey is that sequences of lightning and thunder are not chance occurrences but are events constrained to occur in succession. We give English expression to our recognition of this constraint either

by saying that *lightning causes thunder* or by saying that *if there is lightning, then there will also be thunder.* It has seemed to some philosophers that a *causal nexus*, on the one hand, and a *logical condition*, on the other, are different things, because these alternative statements are not quite equivalent: we do not always hear the thunder that is said to be caused by lightning. A nearer equivalent would be this, *If there is no lightning, then there will be no thunder,* for that is to say that without the *cause*—the first member of the nexus—there can be no *effect*—the second member.

Any example of the logical reasoning which is an alternative to the reasoning processes discussed above, however expressed, can always be reconstructed using the English word *if.* This includes all the reasoning about causal nexus which are at least a great part of the subject matter of Science. The hieroglyphic sentence intended to model *If there is lightning, then there will be thunder* and the account given earlier of its introduction into the language explains its relationship to experience. A sentence constructed with *if* is called by logicians a *hypothetical sentence* and, as we have suggested, gives expression to a constraint that we recognize upon what is possible. We saw above an early example of reasoning by manipulating representations of numbers; we can now consider what may have been the first piece of self-conscious reasoning in the history of Science that seems to be essentially mediated by symbols.

The first mathematicians, who, of course, could reason as well as anyone, found it convenient to distinguish *odd* from *even numbers,* and experience taught them that *odd rectangles have two odd sides* (as we would say, $21 = 3 \times 7$, for example*), and even ones at least one even* ($4 = 2 \times 2$, $6 = 3 \times 2$, and so on). They also found that if an even number could be arranged as a square, then both its sides would be even (as the even square number 36 has sides of even length, 6). By reasoning they could then sometimes exploit what they had learnt without actually arranging pebbles and counting their sides. Considering the number 64, for example, they could reason that s*ince this is an even square number, its sides are even too,* without troubling to count out 64 pebbles and see how they could arrange them in the sand. The hypothetical sentence upon which this piece of reasoning is based is this:

If any square number is even, then its sides are even.

It has two clauses, the one that contains *if* is called the *antecedent*, and the other the *consequent* of the hypothetical sentences. As we have already seen the result of reconstructing a piece of reasoning to make its structure clear typically has an unattractively pedantic feel which is reinforced in the following reconstruction of our original piece about the square number 64 by my avoidance of the use of the pronouns that make our prose flow so smoothly. (I make use of a ruled line just as I did in our model of an analogical argument to separate premisses from conclusion.)

If this square number is even, then the sides of this square number are even.
And indeed, *this square number* **is** *even.*

So, the sides of this square number have to be even.

The modality of the conclusion is now that of logical necessity. There is, however, an important point to the exercise, *viz.* that the reasoning is now as *perspicuous* as it can be: we see exactly what the steps of the argument are. If we assign symbols to recurrent sentences and clauses in this manner,

"This square number is even" > P

"The sides of this square number are even" > Q

and ignore the rhetorical *and even*, we can extract a simple pattern (it was to facilitate this that I shied away from using pronouns). Here it is, the *logical form* of the argument.

If P, then Q
P

So, necessarily Q.

This is quite generally recognized by philosophers as the *canonical model of logical reasoning* (although some like to think that there is a *metaphysical* necessity that is distinct from this *epistemological* variety and so would not allow the "necessarily" to appear here). When it can be extracted from a piece of reasoning, the process of reasoning is said to be the *affirmation of the antecedent of a hypothetical sentence.* Part of the meaning of the English word *if* is shown by exhibiting this form. We find that all passages of reasoning can be reconstructed in either this pattern, or another one which is closely related to it.

On the basis of the experience with collections of pebbles that we have been considering we might, on another occasion, reason as follows with regard to the square number whose sides arc 9.

Since the sides of this square number are not *even, this is not an even number.*

This might be reconstructed in its turn in this manner.

The sides of this square number are even, if this square number is even.

But the sides of this square number are not even

So, this square number cannot be even.

In this case we have to tolerate the disturbingly ungrammatical modality of the hypothetical sentence which, given the *not* is the second premise, should read something like: *The sides of this square number would be even, if this square number were even.* When we also suppress the word *but* a simple pattern is exhibited to complete an account of the meaning of *if*:

If P, then Q

Not Q

So, necessarily not P.

Here we are not affirming the antecedent but rather *denying the consequent of the same hypothetical sentence.* What we are doing in logical reasoning is equivalent to playing the game of arranging sentences of our language in one of these two patterns. (There are certain pieces of reasoning that cannot be accommodated to them, but we need not muddy the waters by noting them here.) If we want to be sure that a piece of reasoning is sound, we attempt to reconstruct it in one of these two canonical forms. We then see exactly what the grounds of our reasoning are: a constraint (the first, *hypothetical* premise: *If P, then Q*) that we suppose ourselves to have recognized, and an assertion or denial (the second, *assertive* premise: either *P,* or *not-Q*) that we suppose ourselves entitled to make. Once we have accepted this logic—*i.e.* this model of logical reasoning—we can criticize what we suppose ourselves to have imagined by considering whether it does observe the constraints we impose on our reasoning. We should not forget, however, in evaluating what our reasoning seems to have taught us that it is *we* who decree that these patterns are canonical. It is another question entirely whether they reflect some reality independent of us (the logical structure of the world, perhaps).

Absurdity

38. The logical critique of imagination is well illustrated by the contribution of Hippasos' to our scientific understanding. The question he asked was this: "Given a square number with sides of some particular length, how long is the side of the square number that is twice the original?" This is, of course, the discrete arithmetical equivalent of the continuous geometrical exercise that Socrates set for Meno's slave. What Hippasos did was to imagine the pebble models of the two numbers side by side (as in the diagram below—in which, however, I have only indicated their boundaries and not the pebbles arranged within them).

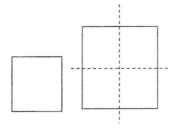

It was when he considered the pebbles within the boundaries and imagined himself counting them that a difficulty emerged. Consider this (recalling that what we mean by an *even* number is one that is twice some other):

> *The original number is either an odd or an even square. Suppose first that it is odd. Then the doubled square contains twice an odd number of pebbles, i.e. it is an even square. Since it is an even square, its sides are also even, and since these sides are even, internal boundaries can be drawn (as shown in my diagram) dividing the number into four identical squares. But now consider two adjacent squares, say the two that make up the lower row. Since they are together twice one and the same number, they are an even rectangular number. But since they are together half the doubled number, they are equal to the original—and so an odd number.*

Had the original number not been odd (as we had Hippasos hypothesize above) but *even*, then it would have been possible to replace all the pebbles, four at a time, with ones of twice the original size, and then to have gone on doing this until the collection had become an odd square, so that he could have conducted us to the same **absurdity**: *that a number should be both odd and even!* Now, it would be exceedingly tedious to do so, but his reasoning could be reconstructed as a chain of arguments in the canonical forms discussed above, so that we could be sure that it contained no errors. What is more important is the *argumentational strategy* of Hippasos which is very characteristic of scientific reasoning. It is known as the **Reductio ad absurdum**. It proceeds by making an hypothesis which is then used as the premise in a valid argument whose conclusion is absurd. Unless it would be less absurd to reject any of the other premises, the absurdity of the conclusion leads us to reject the hypothesis.

The hypothesis in this paradigm of reductive thinking was that, for any given square number, there is a square number which is the original doubled. The absurd conclusion that this number is both odd and even is a confirmation of its contrary: there is no natural number that is both odd and even, so that Hippasos—who was taken out to sea and drowned by his fellow Pythagoreans for this service to Mathematics and Science—has rationally demonstrated that if we can arrange a collection of pebbles as a square, then we will not be able to do the same with a collection of twice as many pebbles. What this means is that the sides of any square and those of its double are *incommensurable*, *i.e.* that a square and its double cannot both be present in the world of experience. The reason he had to be put to death seems to be that he had demonstrated that number (at least as understood by the Pythagoreans, *viz.* as the discrete natural numbers) could not be the foundation of Reality as his fellows believed it to be. A scientist is not a mathematician; he is concerned with concrete empirical reality whilst the mathematician is concerned with what we earlier characterized as an abstract reality. Practically, of course, this result has little interest for the scientist, for a square that is *approximately* double can be present, and that to any desired degree of accuracy. But what Hippasos has done is to derive this very surprising constraint upon **empirical reality** by considering the properties of the **unseen reality** of numbers. He seems to have shown us that what is *present* is constrained by what is not.

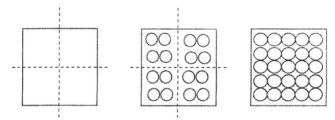

Hippasos' discovery illustrates the *heuristic efficacy* of exploring the symmetry of a problem. In his case, as in many others, this led directly to interesting insight, for the symmetry of a geometrical square is clearly not the same as that of a collection of objects arranged in a square. As the diagram above makes clear whilst any *geometrical* square has axes of symmetry that bisect each pair of opposite sides, and an even-square numbered collection of objects shares this symmetry, no odd-numbered collection does unless one allows objects to be split into parts. In that case, however, the objects would not be the ultimate constituents of Reality, which was precisely the rôle envisaged by the Pythagoreans for their number-atoms.

Theorems

39. We return now to Pythagoras' Theorem. Here is Heath's standard translation of what Euclid actually writes—the text of the **proof** that has beguiled thinking men ever since by its air of irrefutable certainty.

PROPOSITION XLVII

In a right triangle the square drawn on the side opposite the right angle is equal to the squares drawn on the sides that make the right angle.

Let ABC be a right triangle in which CAB is a right angle; then the square drawn on BC is equal to the two squares on CA, AB. On BC draw the square BDEC, and on BA, AC draw the squares GB, HC; through A draw AL parallel to BD or CE; and draw AD and FC. Then, since each of the angles BAG, BAC is a right angle, GA, CA upon meeting BA make the adjacent angles equal to two right angles; therefore AC is in a straight line with GA. For the same reason, BA is in a straight line with AH. And, since angle DBC is equal to angle FBA, because each is a right angle, to each of them add angle ABC; then the whole angle ABD is equal to the whole angle FBC. And since FB is equal to BA, and DB to BC, the two sides FB, BC are equal to the two sides AB, BD respectively; and we proved that angle FBC is equal to angle ABD; therefore triangle FBC is equal to triangle ABD. Furthermore, the parallelogram BL is double the triangle ABD, because they are on the same base BD and in the same parallels BD, AL. And the square GB is double the triangle FBC, because they are on the same base FB and in the same parallels FB, GC. But doubles of the equal triangles FBC, ABD are equal to one another. Therefore the square GB is equal to the parallelogram BL. In the same way, by drawing AE, BK, we could show that the square HC is equal to the parallelogram CL. Therefore the whole square BDEC is equal to the two squares GB, HC. And the square BDEC is drawn on BC, and the squares GB, HC on BA, AC. Therefore the square drawn on BC is equal to the two squares on BA, AC. Therefore, *in a right triangle the square drawn on the side opposite the right angle is equal to the squares drawn on the sides that make the right angle.*

Q.E.D.

Interpretation

40. Here we have what is particularly associated with Euclid's name: a logically co-ordinated series of hypotheses, resting on the bedrock of what is so trivial that it cannot be doubted. The prosaic language is so clear that there can be no mistaking his meaning and neither can there be any doubt about the logical connexions between his assertions (they could all have been reduced to the canonical forms discussed above). But observe this: Euclid actually begins (as he always does) by instructing us in making a construction to be *the model for his words*. None of the several thousand editions of Euclid's Elements that have appeared was without the pictures.

Had we had a version without pictures we should not have understood anything without making a drawing for ourselves with Euclid's text open in front of us. We should already have understood the words of course, *i.e.* we would have known what we were required to do, but until we had carried out the instructions—until we had *done* what the words demand—we should have understood nothing more. We certainly cannot construct anything of comparable complexity in *imagination*. The drawing below is just one that has resulted from following his instructions. But there are other drawings—there is an infinity of them, because Euclid does not tell us how to orient the first triangle on the paper, how large to make its sides, or even the proportions amongst them.

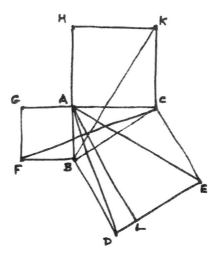

His proof is not then about the picture that is found ready drawn in the book, nor about any other particular picture; it is about a whole *type* of pictures of which this drawing is just one *token*. To grasp Pythagoras' Theorem, then, something more is required than merely to follow Euclid's words in making the drawing: we must also *see* this picture as something Protean that is not just itself but also all the numberless other drawings of the same type. It has already been remarked that no picture can, of itself, show us how it is intended to be seen; only words can do that. And, of course, no picture could show us what was intended to be done with it: that is precisely what the words of Euclid's text have to accomplish. We see then the distinct rôles of the picture and the words: the picture is the *semantic component* and the words the *syntactical component* of a single syntactico-semantic whole. Neither conveys anything to us without the other. The *syntactical* part could have no meaning aside from what is supplied, first, by the semantics of English which we have already considered, and, secondly, by our active doing.

Axiomatization

41. We saw in the last chapter certain very general trivialities concerned with wholes and their parts which had to be relied upon in arriving at the insight contained in Pythagoras Theorem. There are further more specifically geometrical trivialities upon which the whole Euclidean edifice is built. These are observations of certain things that, as draughtsmen, we can certainly *do*. We can:

using a straight edge, draw a line between any two points;

extend such a line indefinitely in either direction;

draw a circle with a pair of compasses with any radius from any point as its centre.

Euclid also observes that when we draw *right angles*, these are always the same, and that a line through a point offset from a given line will intersect that line except in the case of a unique *parallel*. He is then in reality concerned with what we can draw and his aim seems to be to teach us how to draw each of the five Platonic solids. Why should this be so important?—Because, as is clear from Plato's own writings, the Greeks were sensitive to the particular beauty, *mathematical beauty*, manifest in these things and supposed, indeed, that understanding of Reality was somehow inherent in it. This to our minds strangely mystical attitude is something from which later thinkers had to emancipate themselves before the scientific analysis of the empirical world could begin.

These important, fundamental trivialities constitute the **axioms** of Euclid's Geometry. He tells us at the beginning of his book just how he *intends* the words that are crucial to understanding them are to be interpreted: a *point* he writes is what has no dimension, a *line,* is a curve that lies evenly upon itself, and so on. We call these words *theoretical terms* because their meaning is explicitly given in definitions and not merely received usage. We needed nothing more to interpret the text of Euclid's proof of Pythagoras' Theorem and to make the Windmill Drawing with which it is concerned. It is one thing to be sure that his argument is in order (as we find no reason not to be, since we feel that should we be so inclined, we could demonstrate its agreement with our canonical models of logical reasoning), but quite another to be certain that it also constitutes a proof of the theorem. There are two more things required for that, the first being the assurance that the system of axioms is *consistent*. And what that means is that provided our reasoning is correct they could never lead us into any contradiction. (That our reasoning is correct is the second thing.)

Here is a simple *syntactical object* (a text) that declares itself to be a theory and will serve to illustrate what is at issue.

A Theory

Any two PUNKS BUNK only one LUNK; at least two
PUNKS BUNK any LUNK; and there are at least three
PUNKS that do not all BUNK the same LUNK.

You may be inclined to regard this text as nonsensical, if for no other reason than that it contains certain words which do not appear to have their usual English meanings (indeed they seem not to function as their accustomed parts of speech). But I have only to interpret these terms for you and then show you the semantic object (the model) that I intend you to associate with it to dispel this opinion. The model having been presented the meanings of the odd words I used in formulating the theory (its *theoretical terms*) are sufficiently indicated by observations of its structure. Here it the model.

What has to be observed is all the following:

A, B, C, D, E, F and G are PUNKS;

ABC, CDE, EFA, BGE, CGF, AGD and BDFB are LUNKS;

A, B and C BUNK *ABC, C, D and E* BUNK *CDE, and so on.*

This having been done we see that the ink marks on the paper do indeed give the text an intelligible meaning. This material construction supplements the original text to complete a syntactico-semantic whole. You may not find my theory particularly interesting, but it is certainly not nonsense: once all its words have been understood, there can be no denying that it is a *coherent* piece of English prose. It becomes more interesting if the puzzling terms are now re-interpreted by translating each into another English word in this manner:

PUNK > "point"

LUNK > "line"

BUNK > "belong"

because what we then have is part of a formulation of the axiomatic system which a modern mathematician might—constrained by the more exacting standards of contemporary logic—actually use in a presentation of Euclid's geometry, *viz.* the following:

Euclid's Theory

(1) Any two points are contained in only one line;

(2) There are at least two points on every line ;

(3) There are at least three points that do not lie on a single line.

---

he theorems of Euclidean Geometry can be derived from these axioms by logical reasoning and we arrive at an important sense in which the word "model" is used in discussions of scientific method. What we want to say is that these Euclidean axioms are *modelled* by the geometrical drawing above when it is understood that the points on the black lines are the only points there are (so that the black lines are also the only lines there are) whilst the physical points constituting the surface are not part of the model at all. This is not by any means what Euclid *intended* by his system of axioms: BDFB, for example, is not what he meant by a *line*. Interpreted as a model of Euclid's geometry this is, then, a *non-iconic* model—it does not look like what it represents—and it is not, of course, a complete model, for such a thing would have to contain elements to be the representatives of an *infinite* number of points. (Indeed, it does not give any meaning to the other axioms, such as *"Any three points lie on a plane*," that are needed to produce all of Euclid's results). What it is, then, is a **partial model** of Euclid's axiomatic system. A "model" in this final sense is a material object that shows a system of postulates to be *consistent* in the sense that individual material objects are *consistent*: their parts fit together to constitute a whole; they have no feature that is not compatible with each of the others. And that is exactly what is achieved by *modelling* the axioms in the way we have just done. I began with the meaningless terms PUNK, LUNK and BUNK to show that it is through this process that the theoretical terms actually acquire the meanings they must be given if the text is to constitute a proof.

Formal Logic

42. Merely *looking* at a model of this kind shows us that what the theory says is not only meaningful but also *consistent*. The material world is the only reality we know, so that nothing could be more real to us than the things it contains. Amongst these is a quite specific *material object* that is exactly described by the axioms of a theory (the drawing) so that Euclid's theory, insofar as it is grounded upon these axioms, fits together as well as does the material world in which we lead our lives. But the other thing alluded to above that must be assured before we can have confidence in Euclid's theorems is the reasoning that is applied to the axioms. This must, it seems, be shown to be consistent in the same way, *i.e.* we must produce some material object that will convince us of its consistency. The object chosen by the mathematicians concerned with this problem is the **set**.

What we are to understand by the word "set" is any collection of things. In the case of portable material things of reasonable size we could make a set out of them by circumscribing an area on the ground and placing all the things destined to be its **members** inside (these together comprise the **extension** of the set in logical jargon). Now, as has been remarked, the primary function of language is to categorize things. The business of categorization is the basis of the mathematician's model of human reasoning. We have in our language the word "bison" (and our model hieroglyphic language has suggested where it ultimately came from by its adoption of the word "🐃"). This set might be represented in the manner of the drawing below. (A horse is also shown which, of course, in not a member of this set and so is outside the circumscribed area.)

But the mathematician is concerned with logical principles which abstract from specific types of things and so represent only things in general. The pictures of sets he actually uses are accordingly more on the lines of the next drawing.

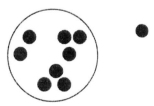

In this representation we are no longer shown what the members of the set are but we can elaborate the picture to show the relationships upon which logical reasoning depends.

Suppose now that we concentrate upon just one individual bison. The drawing to the left below shows some uncategorized individual as a member of some set to which it belongs. This having been grasped, what the right-hand drawing shows is some individual excluded from a set to which it does not belong. In the formal logic of the Twentieth Century the first drawing is the semantic basis of a fundamental sentence, one that is then represented by a sentence variable such as p or q. Such a sentence ascribes some property (*e.g.* being a bison) to some particular thing. The drawing to the right denies some such sentence so that its meaning can be represented by modifying a sentence variable with some symbol which thus acquires the same meaning as the English word "not," in this manner: $\neg p$.

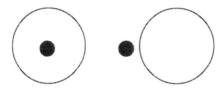

Similarly, the drawing to the left immediately below provides the semantics for sentences of the same logical type as, "This is a bull and that is a cow," any token of which can be represented with the introduction of a further symbol in this manner, $p \wedge q$, to be interpreted with the English word "and." The semantics for another of the many meanings that "and" has in English is provided by the drawing to the right, which shows some individual as a member of two different sets (perhaps those of bison and male animals, respectively).

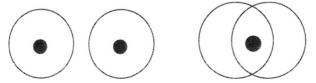

Suppose now that the outer circle in the drawings below contains all the members of the set labelled by the English word "animal," then a sub-set (as one says) can

be formed which contains only those animals that are also bison. The two sets—
the *animal*-set and its *bison* sub-set—are both shown in the second drawing.

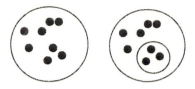

Given the interpretation I intended what this picture now shows is that *if* a thing is
a bison, *then* it is also an animal. But what the un-interpreted picture can be said
to show is just the logical relationship which is given expression in English by a
sentence of the form *if p, then q*. Introducing one further symbol we can write the
formula $p \supset q$ to be given this meaning. (More precisely this picture supplies the
semantics for the *if ... then...* relationship only insofar as it connects simple
predicative sentences such as *This is a bison* or *This is an animal*. In the more
general case a rather different model is needed, for example one in which points
on a plane surface are labelled with the letters p, q, and so on, and arrows are
drawn between certain pairs of labelled points.) This is the relationship that is the
basis of the *modus ponens* and *modus tollens* that we considered above. The
symbol "⊦" is used to separate a list of formulæ representing the premises in
arguments from the conclusions they jointly entail, so that these *modi* are
represented by the following pair of symbolic sentences:

$$p, \ p \supset q \vdash q$$
$$\neg q, \ p \supset q \vdash \neg p$$

Details is lacking in this summary but we nevertheless glimpse how the notion of
"set" can provide the semantic component of a theory of logic—a theory like
Euclid's geometry that can be cast into axiomatic form. This "calculus" is the
modern canonical model of deduction. Drawings like those I have just shown you
can then supply the material object needed to confirm the consistency of such a

logical calculus, so that both of our requirements for accepting the certainty of Euclid's demonstrations can seem to have been met.

Paradox

43. But things are not really so simple. The members of a set can be any things at all, including mathematical objects and other abstractions. The only constraint would seem to be that we should be able to specify precisely which things are included in it. If we could not do this, then our attempt would be something diffuse upon which our powers of reasoning would gain no hold. Thus there is no reason not to make a set out of *all sets which are not members of themselves*. This set has just been specified in a grammatically well-formed English sentence so that it would seem to satisfy our criterion. But as Bertrand Russell—the diabolical progenitor of this notorious set—points out it is a paradoxical object because its own relationship to itself is incomprehensible. We might try saying that it is a member of itself but then the specification leaves no doubt that it is not a member of itself. It seems, then, that we must say that it is not a member of itself, but then, as the specification makes no less clear, that is exactly what it is. The paradoxical nature of this set led Russell himself to conclude that it is not enough that the extension of a set should be capable of grammatically well-formed specification for a putative set really to be one; what was needed in addition was a *hierarchical typification* that would ensure that sets of things, on the one hand, and those things themselves, on the other, would belonging to different levels of the hierarchy of types and could not both be members of one and the same set. This would indeed make a non-set of any *set which is a member of itself*, so that the pretended specification of the extension of the Russell Set thereby became nonsense. But from our perspective the real significance of the Russell set is that its specification is already nonsense because it is cut loose from any possible semantics. We cannot make any non-linguistic representation of a *set which is a member of itself* as may be clear from the failed attempt to do so below. Only words could explain what I suppose myself to be doing in this picture—and those words could have no

semantics and so would be meaningless. This failure is dignified as the *Paradox of Self-reference*; we see here the fundamental move of self-bafflement that is the ever present enemy of science.

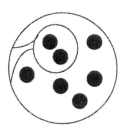

Undecidability

44. Russell's hierarchy is an *ad hoc* solution to one pernicious manifestation of self-bafflement but it hardly helps with another. The French mathematician Jules Richard contrives something no less fiendish with a list of arithmetical definitions. Here is an extract from a list (not Richard's original) that would have served his purpose:

1. An even number is one divisible by 2;

2. An odd number is one that is not even;

3. A prime number has no factors other than 1 and itself;

4. A square number is the product of a number with itself;

5. ...

A *Richardian number* is now defined as one to which the property specified in the proposition indexed by it *does not apply*. Thus the number 1, in not being even, is Richardian as is the number 2, whilst numbers 3 and 4 are non-Richardian in that they are prime and square numbers, respectively. The notion of Richardianism is self-reflexive in the sense that it is at least as much about the list as it is about numbers; nevertheless, it does seem to be as well defined as any of the other properties on the list. It should then be added to the list as, let us say, its 5th item:

5. A Richardian number is one to which the property defined by the proposition indexed by it on this list does not apply.

And here is a paradox to place alongside Russell's, for this definition makes it clear that the number 5 is Richardian only if it has the property of being non-Richardian whilst it is not Richardian only if it is. The number falls under the definition only if it does not and *vice versa*. Thus despite being in possession of a clear definition we are not in a position to decide whether 5 is Richardian or not.

It is this quality of *undecidability* that attracts Gödel's attention. He studies Richard's construction as though it were the model of a mathematical theory, each definition on the list being the counterpart in this model of a proposition that might be a theorem of the theory. He then considers the counterpart of the paradoxical item: it might itself be a theorem, but since its paradoxical nature consists in its entailing its own contradiction, the theory would then be inconsistent; alternatively, that contradiction might itself be a theorem, but (since it too has the same paradoxical nature) that again would make the theory inconsistent. The only way a theory could be consistent would then be that neither the paradoxical counterpart nor its contradiction should be theorems, *i.e.* that the theory should not be powerful enough to decide between them. If the theory modelled by Richard's list were *consistent*, then, it would also be *incomplete*. The point of disanalogy is, of course, that the fifth definition can seem to be an unnecessary item: it does not define a genuine arithmetical property but is rather an *ad hoc* contrivance designed to generate paradox. What Gödel has in mind as the counterpart of this item in the modelled theory is a proposition that belongs to the proper province of the theory—he has conceived of the *Gödelian proposition*.

Richard's trick was to make an item on his list refer to the list itself. What Gödel now does is to make arithmetic capable of self-reference in an analogous manner. He finds the means in the bizarre practices of numerology by which, in one famous example, the biblical *Number of the Beast* is 666 (and, presumably, the equally remarkable DCLVI in the Vulgate) and is arrived at by allowing the letters spelling out a certain Hebrew word simultaneously to have the values they do when they are given their alternative use as numerals. Only the most determined non-specialist could be interested in following the details of what is known as *Gödel's Proof* but, in very summary outline, what he now does is this. He uses numbers to encode the individual symbols of formal logic (the p's, q's, ¬'s, ⊢'s, ⊃'s, and so on, that were discussed above) and also all strings of symbols including those that constitute not just logical formulæ but also entire mathematical proofs. Each symbol, formula and proof has its own Gödelian number, but the numbers he uses for the individual symbols are prime numbers. Now, we saw earlier how a number can be factorized to extract its prime factors but without emphasizing that this factorization is *unique*—there is only one list of the prime factors of any given number. This means that the symbols which constitute a formula can be recovered from its Gödelian number. Gödel also arranges things to ensure that these symbols are recovered in their correct order, so that each natural number corresponds to a logical expression.

The little that has now been said may be enough to make Gödel's achievement comprehensible. The proof of any proposition is a sequence of formulæ which ends with the proposition itself. It is plausible, then, that the existence of a proof for a given proposition is a particular relation between two numbers (the Gödelian number of the proposition and the Gödelian number of its proof). Any general relationship between two numbers is a proper part of Arithmetic and Gödel succeeds in making this particular arithmetical relationship explicit. He then performs Richard's trick—except that it is no longer sleight of hand, for it is concerned with nothing other than precisely arithmetical relationships. He writes down the celebrated Gödelian Formula and calculates its Gödelian number. Let us say that this number is g. What the Gödelian Formula says is this: *there is no proof of the arithmetical formula with Gödelian number g*. Like any other arithmetical proposition, *e.g.* 2+2=4 or 2+2=5, this formula must either be an arithmetical truth or else be arithmetically false. What we see, however (and here the paradoxical whimsicality of Richard's construction becomes something unimpeachably mathematical), is that if the Gödelian formula has a proof, then it has none, whereas (and this is the only alternative) if it has no proof then it does have one. Our logic and our arithmetic are not powerful enough to decide this arithmetical question: the Gödelian Formula is *formally undecidable* and so our theory is *incomplete*. However, the arithmetical formula with Gödelian number g is actually a truth of Arithmetic, and Gödel proves this by other, *informal* means.

What are we to make of this?—Well, this is claimed to be a demonstration that there is more to mathematical thinking than can be captured in any axiomatic system on the lines of Euclid's geometry. Mathematics is concerned with abstractions; if this is true of mathematical thinking that it is certainly true of scientific thinking which is concerned with the untidy concrete things of human experience. There is more to scientific thinking as indeed we see just by considering Gödel's own thought. I presented this—quite fairly, as it seems to me—as essentially an exercise in *analogical* thinking, that is to say as a recognition of the sameness in two disparate representations (Richard's sly list, on the one hand, and a formal arithmetical theory, on the other).

Summary

45. This chapter has explained the way in which the apparent deliverances of insight are *warranted* by the mathematician, something which concerns us because, as we shall see, it is also some part of the way of the scientist. We began by considering the games of counting, which provides the semantics for our numerals, and of the geometrical arrangement of tokens, which is the basis of all discrete mathematics. The question of whether numbers are anything more than artefacts of these games was touched upon but our purpose was rather to illuminate the process of rational *confirmation* by revisiting its origins in Ancient Greece. To this end the notion of an *hypothesis* or non-gratuitous supposition, typically founded upon experiment, was introduced. It was explained that Science, like mathematics, is vitally concerned with the *rational confirmation* of hypotheses and the *coherent ampliation* of those that have been confirmed. The modes of reasoning employed to this end—*analogical*, *inductive* and *logical*

reasoning—were demonstrated and the notion of *canonical models* of rational processes explained at length. Special attention was then paid to Euclid's theory of Geometry; his proof of the Pythagorean Theorem was examined to display the *axiomatic structure* of the whole theory. The important idea of constructing a material interpretation of such a structure (a *model* of it in, as was explained, another sense of the term) to confirm its consistency was introduced. This idea was then applied to an axiomatization of the canonical model of the process of logical reasoning presented earlier by using set-theoretical diagrams as a model to confirm its consistency. Finally, a somewhat summary account was offered of the reasons why the hope that the consistency of theories had been secured in this way is now recognized as mere illusion. There is more to rational thinking than logical deduction; precisely because this was not understood by philosophers of Science in the Twentieth Century and their followers at the beginning of the Twenty-First, it is our aim in this essay is to uncover what more there may be.

REPRESENTATION

Models

46. We are strongly inclined to accept without question Euclid's notion of a *line*: such an entity consists, so he tells us, of the points that lie evenly upon it, and these are so dense that a third point lies between any two, no matter how close together they might. The consequence of this—since it is also part of the same notion that a line can be extended in either direction without end—is that there is an endless number of points lying *along* a line but also an endless number of points *between* any two of them. Once this is spelt out it almost seems incomprehensible but there is a way of representing lines which made it seem reasonable, or even obvious. All we have to do is to imagine the points on the line being *projected* onto another line.

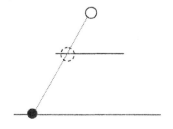

In the diagram above the original line is the lower of the two parallel lines and there is also a fixed point not on either of the pair. Given any point lying on the original line (the black circle in the diagram) we can join it to the fixed point and clearly there will be a point (within the stippled circle in the diagram) on the shorter line where the constructed line intersects it. Since this can be done with any point on the first line, what the diagram shows us is that there are as many points in the shorter line as there are in the longer one. If we now bend the shorter line as shown in the next diagram and choose the point of projection appropriately then we see that there are, indeed, as many points in any line (no matter how short) as there are in one that goes on all the way to the infinite bounds of Space!

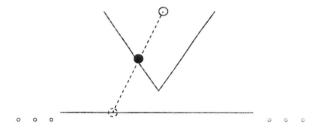

As reasonable beings we will not allow ourselves to say that this cannot be so, because the diagrams plainly show us that it is. What we can do, of course, is to reject the Euclidean notion and say, for example, that what we meant by "line" was, rather, something comprising a very large fixed number of very small points. "Line" is one of the fundamental theoretical terms of Euclid's geometrical theory and what is illustrated by all this is the inter-relatedness of such terms, on the one hand, and our representations of their meanings, on the other. In our systematic thinking, be it in mathematics or in more general scientific use, the only way we can know what we are talking about is by making a *representation* of what we say. The diagrams above supply the *semantics* for Euclid's technical use of the word "line."

The representation provided by the first diagram is *iconic* in that what it represents it does so without any reliance upon *convention*. The representation provided by the second, however, exploits the fundamental conventional device of using dots to indicate an indefinite continuation of the same. Such a convention has its own semantic basis which must be appropriated before its contribution to the representation can be grasped. Without employing a convention we cannot picture an *infinite* line but we can construct what it seems appropriate to term a finite "model" of one by projecting each of the points on the line from the north pole, as it were, onto the circumference of a circle resting on the line by what would then be its south pole, as in the next diagram. It is the circle and not the rest of the diagram that constitutes the model and its particular virtue is that the points at the ends of the line—the points at infinity—are represented in it. A new oddness emerges in that the representatives of the points at opposite ends of the line are one and the same point in the model, *viz.* the north pole. We are reminded by this that a model is not its own original. There will be *points of disanalogy* between the two and it is the use to which we put the model that decides whether these are acceptable. (Mathematicians do find good use for this particular model.)

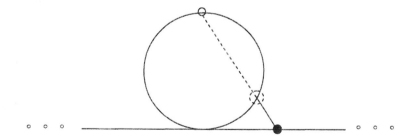

Spurious Models

47. Whereas Science is the attempt to understand the world of experience, Mathematics is a game with no concern beyond itself. However, as our example

suggests, Mathematics too has a use for models that are concrete in the sense that they could, in principle at least, be constructed out of the stuff we have for hand in the world of our experience. The particular case of the mathematical innovations of Cantor shows how such a concrete model can provide the semantics for new symbols. He can be seen as meeting the scientist half way, for in doing science concrete models are made which must be suited to the application of existing mathematical symbols.

The most mysterious property of the numbers we have playfully brought into being is their *infinity*: just like Euclidean lines they go on and on forever. To grasp this mystery we must produce some model of it. "Infinity" is the name of a point on our circular model of the line but that hardly helps us to manipulate it as a number. We get nowhere by trying to construct it with collections of pebbles; what can seem to serve, however, is to mark individual pebbles with our numerals so that each becomes a counter that can represent a number.

We now need something to contain our counters. The box illustrated in the drawing below with the places themselves numbered from 1 to 6 would certainly not do because it has room for six counters but none for even a seventh, never mind all the others which will have to be accommodated.

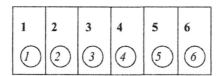

We can try to make a model of the box that would serve by thinking that we do the following: we pick up the first counter and put it into the box; then we do the same with the next counter, and so on, but each time we put a new counter into the box, we move all the counters already there up one place to make room for it.

But such a suggestion is not really a *model* at all. Nothing made of the stuff and in the space and time of our experience could have the capacity never to be full and so always to have room for one more counter. However, Cantor clearly has in mind something rather like an infinitely long box; it is suggested (but, again, hardly more than so) in the next drawing. This time each place in the box is supposed to be numbered up to and including the last, up to and including, that is, the number reached after we have exhausted all our numerals. There is, of course, no numeral provided by our counting-game to name this the number that comes after the last so Cantor invents one, $\aleph_0$ (pronounced *aleph-nought* in the English-speaking world), recruiting the first letter in the Hebrew alphabet.

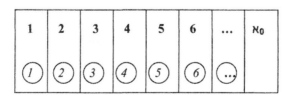

The conventional dots are, of course, to suggest all the places whose numbers are not explicitly shown. We are to understand that there are now enough compartments in the box for any number of counters. We say that with the introduction of $\aleph_0$ there is now an infinity of numerals, or (in the jargon of mathematicians) that $\aleph_0$ is the *cardinality of infinity* i.e. the number of numbers there would be in a *completed infinity*. This then is *Cantor's model of infinity*: it is the semantic model that makes the mathematician's discourse about a discrete infinity meaningful, or at least enables him to claim that it is. But what understanding of the notion does it afford us?

Suppose the compartments to be numbered following Cantor's proposal, but suppose also that we have two complete sets of counters. We arrange our counters in the box in the fashion shown in the next diagram.

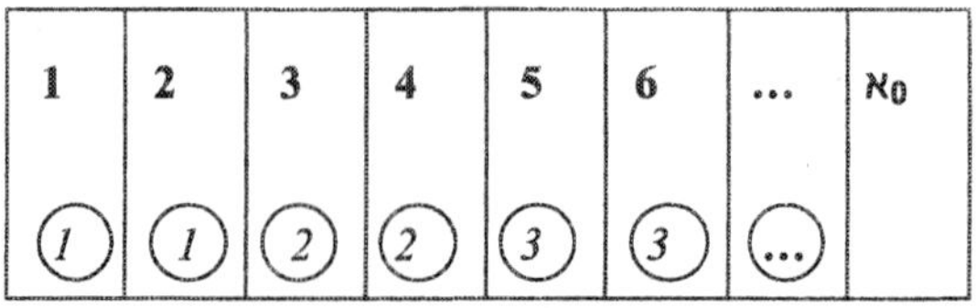

The odd thing—the utterly incomprehensible thing—is that because there is an *infinity* of places (*i.e.* a place for everything we could *count*), there must be room in the box for all our counters (and not for half as many as what we call *common sense* would very strongly prompt us to believe)! Cantor's box has become a model of the natural numbers with which we count, but it hardly helps us to *understand* because we cannot see what is going on in the dotted portion of the drawing. It seems to show us that twice infinity is no more than infinity, a result that is symbolized as follows in Cantor's strange arithmetic of what are called *transfinite numbers*:

$$2\aleph_0 = \aleph_0!$$

But we have hardly begun with the counter-intuitive strangeness of infinity. Much as it seemed clear before we began that two infinities of counters must be more than just one, it seems clear that there are far more fractional numbers than there are integers.

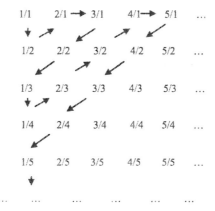

However, if we make counters marked with all our fractional numbers (including the integers written as fractions: 1/1 for 1, 2/1 for 2, and so on), then we will be able to arrange them in the two-dimensional array shown here using the same device of iterated dots. But having arranged the counters in this manner we can trace the continuous path indicated in the drawing through the array and having done that stretch it out like a concertina with all the counters now in a single row.

$$1/1 \quad 1/2 \quad 2/1 \quad 3/1 \quad 2/2 \quad 1/3 \quad 1/4 \quad 2/3 \quad 3/2 \quad \ldots$$

This path includes all the fractions but we see that they can be put into our box in the usual way: contrary to our unmodelled intuition, then there are only countably many fractions. There is an infinity of rows in the scheme and also an infinity of columns so that it seems that infinity multiplied by itself is still only infinity:

$$\aleph_0{}^2 = \aleph_0!$$

What Cantor has given us is, of course, a model of *completed infinity*; his model makes this notion available for our thought (it supplies a semantics for the word "infinity") and it is the basis of an extension of Arithmetic which, however strange, is perfectly consistent. Whether this is what we mean by "infinity" is quite another matter. It might now seem that $\aleph_0$ (the number of numbers in a completed infinity) is the *biggest* number of all, which would explain to some extent why no matter what we do with it, it never gets any bigger. But what are we to call the number of points in a line. Perhaps it should be $\aleph_1$ but we cannot be sure that there are not other very big numbers in between, one of which should then be given the next name after $\aleph_0$. Transfinite arithmetic has an answer to propose, but unless we are confident that we have really been shown a model that represents these notions, we are no longer listening.

Space

48. In a picture things are organized in Space. It is the space of the picture that brings *Space* into being—much as the Greek play with pebbles on the beach did the same for *Number*.

As we have just been reminded by our geometrical and arithmetical reflections the problem with the Space that is thereby brought into being is its *infinity* and *continuity*: it goes on and on forever, so that we could never reach its ends, and is so compact that we could never pull it apart. I have insisted that we have no understanding of anything in our experience without having made some representation of it. There can, however, seem to be a limitation to what we can model. Infinity may well lie beyond but the fundamental limit is this: that *we can*

make no representation of the medium in which we make our representation. Thus it is difficult to see what a model of *Matter* could possibly be, since Matter is the stuff out of which the model would have to be made. And it is no less difficult to see what a model of Space might be, since Space is that within which the stuff of the model would have to be arranged. A model cannot *represent* Matter but only *present* it; in the same way no model could represent Space but only occupy some part of it. Models of Space or Matter are, then, more *representatives* than *representations.* If we should be tempted to view the sheet of paper shown in the drawing below as the model of part of one plane in Space, then it would only be in a convoluted sense in which a *presentation is a self-representation*—the same sense in which the sheet is also a representation of matter.

We can, however, use the matter at hand in the world of our experience to show ourselves how this world might have been different. Euclid has shown us how Space is to be conceived of as the structure within which certain figures can be drawn (in particular, triangles and circles). If we can grasp this thought, then we can also grasp the thought that the figures we can draw might have been other than they are—that more than one straight line might have joined a single pair of points, for example, or that a single line might have intersected the same point more than once. The partial model of Space that I am exhibiting here is marked with a triangle. It is a feature of Euclid's space that the sum of the angles of this triangle is two right-angles, and also that it has many properties which appear so obvious that it seems perverse even to mention them: thus it does not intersect itself and it has an inside and an outside which would, had my model been big enough, have extended indefinitely to the edges of Space and not merely of my piece of paper. Another space of such strange symmetry in which other axioms applied is a possibility that we can be said to grasp only to the extent we can produce a model of the non-Euclidean space (as it would then be natural to say) in which they did apply. However, this model could not but be some material thing contained within the Euclidean space of our experience.

Antinomy

49. The reason we might want to think about non-Euclidean spaces (apart from our intellectual curiosity and love of the bizarre) is this: we do not really understand Euclidean space at all. The particular problem is that we do not grasp how it could have no end, but simply go on and on. At the same time we do not grasp how Space could have any limit. The reason the notion of Space is so very puzzling is, of course, that we have no model of it *as a whole*, no more than does Cantor of a completed infinity. What we suppose ourselves to be imagining when we try to model Space is a subtle container—say a box, which is *subtle* in the sense that it is empty and its walls are not made of any stuff. Any boundary to this box would have to isolate it from the rest of another, wider and even subtler container, an outer box, then, that would be real Space and not the counterfeit inner box with which we began—just as any material box we declared to be a model of Space would itself be contained within what it was supposed to represent. We encounter a limit to what we can model in the case of Space, and so a limit to what we can consistently imagine, a limit which, as we shall see, emerges again and again in trying to think about the most fundamental of things. Whenever we encounter it we say to ourselves that this is yet another manifestation of what goes on and on without end and so cannot be encompassed

by the thought of an existent entity. For any space that we can represent to ourselves, there is always one more beyond.

Curved Space

50. Exploiting the matter found within the space of experience we can make models of other, non-Euclidean spaces—or at least of surfaces within such spaces. We do this by taking an object with a flat surface—most conveniently a piece of paper—and "developing" it (as mathematicians say) by applying it to something solid but not itself flat, such as a cylinder or a cone. We do this taking care not to tear or stretch the sheet so that *locally* nothing will have changed, *i.e.* a tiny insect on the piece of paper would not notice that anything had happened. It will help my argument if we suppose this insect to be a geometer, given to drawing lines and triangles at an appropriate scale. If we apply our sheet to a cylinder we will, within the space that seems to us to be Euclidean, have made a model of a surface in, let us say, "Cylinder-Space." This space is locally the same as the space of our experience—so that our insect geometer can draw the same lines and triangles it did on the flat sheet—but on the scale at which *we* make our drawings things are very different: the *intrinsic* geometry of a surface in Cylinder-Space is still Euclidean, but its *extrinsic* geometry is very odd indeed. The experience of our insect geometer is the same as ours, but a description from our situation beyond the cylindrical surface in which we look down upon the insect's world as a philosopher or mathematician tries to view the space of our ordinary experience (and so of our scientific investigations) is quite different.

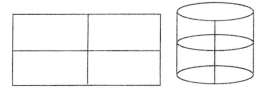

Suppose we had drawn the lines shown in my diagram on the sheet of paper (the "covering") before we wrapped it around the cylinder. We ensure that the sheet of paper is exactly long enough to make a perfect join, so that there is no edge and space is continuous. Both lines are still intrinsically straight, but the one that ran along the length of the sheet of paper has now become endless (so that our insect could crawl along it forever). These orthogonal lines are the extreme cases; in others *i.e.* those of oblique lines, the intrinsically straight lines of the insect geometer spiral up and down the cylinder.

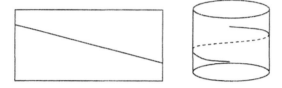

But what we have done so far is only to make the very simplest model of Cylinder-Space, *viz.* a *one-sheeted covering* of the cylinder. Suppose instead that we take a much longer sheet and wrap it around the cylinder several times (it must be supposed to be of sufficiently transparent paper to allow the lines and points in any layer to show through). When we do this the intrinsic space of the insect (which stays, of course, on the outer surface) shows itself to be very odd indeed. A line running the length of the sheet now spirals around the cylinder several times:

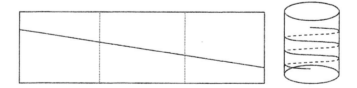

whilst different straight lines converging on a single point can (if their starting points are carefully chosen) become straight lines in the intrinsic geometry of the cylinder that all connect the same two points. In this geometry, then, there is any number of straight lines joining two points.

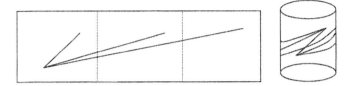

Play with this model will reveal other remarkable properties that we—the external observer comfortably at home in our three-dimensional Euclidean space—will attribute to it. Thus, for example, a sufficiently large triangle in Cylinder-Space will intersect itself, as can be grasped from the diagram below.

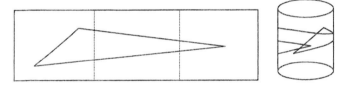

No covering could be made for a sphere out of a non-elastic material such as paper which could then be laid flat for lines to be drawn upon it. What can be done, however, is to roll a ball along a straight line inscribed on the floor in, say, chalk that will then mark the spherical surface of the ball with a line that is intrinsically straight. Such a line will be found to be a great-circle of the sphere— one with its own centre at the centre of the sphere itself. (In the case of our almost spherical planet these are its *geodesics* so the term is used quite generally for the intrinsically straight lines of any curved space.) Considered as the circles they extrinsically are, each has two centres—just as the North- and South-Poles of the earth are both centres of the equator. Everything, indeed, is strangely doubled up: lines in spherical space are endless and there are two paths between any two points along the line connecting them (as there are between England and Australia: one via Europe and the other via the Arctic Ocean); all lines intersect;

the triangles made by three lines are also doubled, one on either side of the sphere, and both the inside and the outside of these triangle are of finite size.

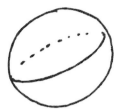 

We live on such a sphere, but the space of our experience is nevertheless locally Euclidean. For all we can tell—for our experience is very, very local on any astronomical scale—the space that contains our world might be as strangely curved as any of the surfaces we have been modelling. Whether this is so is ultimately an *empirical question*, but one which investigation could only ever lead to the answer that within the error of our measurements, the space of experience is Euclidean. We have our *integral models* of surfaces in Cylinder- and Sphere-Space, which is to say that we have some understanding of these spaces as subsistent entities. But we have no more than a *local model* of experiential space (the space of Euclid's *Elements*), which, by the same token, is to say that we have no more understanding of it as a whole than we do of the natural numbers.

Hyperspace

51. The narrative sequence of pictures on the wall of a cave would bring Space and Time into being together: the space within each picture, and the time between them. That the two *together* constitute the phenomenological framework of our experience was the whole basis of Kant's marvellous philosophy but it was only in the last century that models were produced of the unified whole of Space-Time. Because our model of separated Time is, as was remarked earlier, a divided line, the unification is easily accomplished by making Time another dimension to be added to phenomenological Space. The result is a strange sort of space, one which

the mathematician classifies as a *hyperspace* because it has too many dimensions. Phenomenal space has the two dimensions of the flat earth upon which we walk and the third dimension through which things fall and fly. The extraordinary thing that comes as a great surprise when we first catch sight of it is that the space of our imagination is clearly *four*-dimensional. To see this, consider your own house. There is, you will no doubt be inclined to say, a certain picture in your mind, but now explain to yourself just exactly where *you* are in this picture—or, far more to the point, where your *eye* is. In thinking of your house you are both inside and outside simultaneously and everywhere around it and within at one and the same time. You see everything that is going on there up the chimney, under the carpets and inside the darkest cupboards. The house is open to you in *imaginary* perception in quite a different way from that in which it appears in *sensory* perception. It is not a question of your moving about from place to place to catch different three-dimensional glimpses of the building: the whole thing is laid out around you and there is no constraint upon your moving through it. What it means to be able to conceive of things as objects in *three* dimensions is to inhabit *four*— four spatial dimensions, and not the three spatial plus one temporal dimensions of a representation of Space-Time. In fact it becomes clear when you see how readily you can imagine something *happening* in your house (which you can only do by keeping an imaginary eye upon it as imaginary time passes) that the temporal dimension comes in addition to these four.

We *understand* a world of material things disposed in three-dimensional space only because we can make pictures of it, and a picture can be symbolically reduced in the manner of the semantics of our hieroglyphic language. Learning to do so—to picture a three-dimensional world, that is—was the first and, to my mind, the greatest, intellectual accomplishment of the Renaissance that inaugurated the revolution in human thought which is the invaluable contribution of the West to human culture. What we learned to do was to make the perspective drawings in which the third dimension of phenomenal space is *projected* onto the flat surface of a canvas so that (as a very counter-intuitive effect) things of the same size are shown smaller and smaller as they recede into its depths. We cannot perform the same trick with hyperspace; on the other hand, however, we can only understand as much as is shown of hyperspace in our best *two*-dimensional representations of it—which is just as well for an author who relies upon diagrams in discussing such matters.

Space-Time

52. The primitive temporal matrix that provides the semantics for our narratives can easily be exploited to show the movement of material things through phenomenal space. Here is a series of pictures showing a sun with its satellite. "The planet is here, then here, then here," we might say, moving our attention from each picture to the next.

I have suggested the orbit of the planet with a stippled line and to get my meaning you have to interpolate between the pictures and animate the whole in your imagination to send the planet on its way along this path. In the case of a situation as essentially planar as this I can also represent the motion in a unified space-time. To do this I must—in imagination—take my pictures and heap them up upon one another to form the tower shown below. I can incorporate a continuous succession of other pictures between each pair and the structure I have then built will be as solidly three-dimensional as your house and open to the four-dimensional eye of imagination in just the same way. Within this tower we see a stationary sun that appears as a column running the height of the whole, whilst the orbit of the planet is a spiral centred upon it.

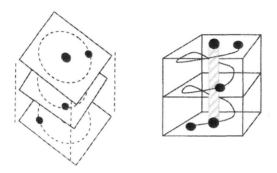

This is the best intuitive representation of a restricted part of Space-Time that we can manage. To represent the whole we can draw a circle and tell ourselves that it is the satisfactorily endless three-dimensional space of our experience in its entirety and make it the circumference of one cross-section of a cylinder of infinite length whose growing height we shall say is the passage of phenomenal time (which is what I intend to suggest in the first drawing below).

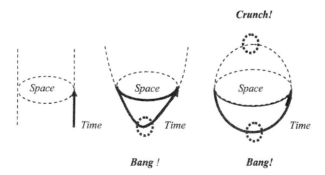

But a time which had no first moment and which will have no last is the affront to our understanding that we noted previously—as unreasonable, in being impossible to model, as a Space with boundaries. We must give Time its provisional beginning by identifying the event with which it begins (the Big Bang of popular imagination) with the coming-into-being of Space. We then arrive at the most satisfying intuition of Space-Time in the manner of the second drawing in which Space expands, *as it were*, to accommodate the phenomenal world. "As it were," for there is nothing for Space to expand into but a further dimension supplied by the same imagination that sees into and through material things. We are no more satisfied with a Time that goes on forever than one that has no beginning, so we must, in this same imagination bring it to a provisional halt (the Crunch) in which final event there is no longer any Space. What we then hold onto in imagination is the three-dimensional sphere shown in the final drawing.

But this will not do. We no more comprehend a Space that comes into being than one that no longer is. The only representation of Space-Time that can appeal to the scientific imagination is one in which the beginnings and ends of Space and Time are somehow all one. And we can manipulate our model to make this so. We depress the poles of our sphere as though we were intent on making a torus, but rather than piercing it we allow the points which were the Great Bang and the Crunch to become one (the process suggested in two stages below).

This representation is, however, of no use at all if we see it as *dynamic*. What we are required to do is to see it is a *static* structure. Space-Time is not something that evolves in Time: it simply subsists! And that is the very great—perhaps insurmountable—difficulty for our comprehension. Ours is a world of single moments each of which arrives to impress itself upon human consciousness before giving way to the next and which, until it does give way, is all there is to phenomenal reality. But if Space-Time is taken for Reality then this is a delusion, for all the moments that ever were, or ever might have been, or ever might be open to human consciousness are elements of one and the same eternally immutable thing. Such is the fundamental scientific conception of Reality. A metaphysician might come to the same conclusion and one readily thinks of Nietzsche with his doctrine of Eternal Recurrence, but his thinking is based upon an intuition of a quite different—and so unscientific—nature, one for which there is no concrete model.

Automation

53. The above were all models for *static* contemplation in that they derived from intuitions of the Space and Time which together are the theatre in which our doings and the events we experience happen. The action in this theatre can only be represented in models which are *dynamic*. In these pages I have consistently represented human beings as creatures who make pictures and reduce them to symbols; in this perspective the most interesting events to be represented are those episodes of mental activity in which we play with our symbols. We can do better than simply to show one of our fellows performing a calculation by having the same event happening both *inside his head* and on a sheet of paper *outside* in his hands. We can consider the rules he seems to be following as he goes along (that is to say the rules we would be following were we the calculator).

Turing has a way of representing mental activity as play regulated by *rules* that are, at least on occasion, so simple that it is possible to conceive of the players not as thinking human beings but as *automata* entirely lacking in human mentality. The famous automaton Turing imagined was a device that would, at a given moment, be in one of a repertoire of different *states* in the sense that it would be following a particular set of rules. These rules would constrain what it did with an endless tape that was presented to it. Turing can be supposed to have imagined (and perhaps also drawn) the picture below in which the automaton is shown with its tape divided into cells each of which may or may not be marked. (The dots are to suggest that the tape goes on forever.)

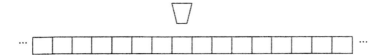

The imaginary game-playing automaton would start in its *initial state* and before taking any action would first determine whether the cell confronting it was marked. Having done so, the rules that comprised its being in that state would determine its action. It would mark or unmark the cell or perhaps leave it unchanged; it would move left or right to the next cell or else stay put; and having done any of these it might change its own state so that it would then proceed by following a different set of rules. The instantaneous situation of the automaton can be pictured by showing it with a number identifying its current state and either marking the cell beneath it or leaving it unmarked.

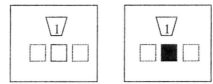

(It is a useful convention that a cell shown with a stippled outline is not determinately either marked or unmarked.) The representation of a rule would then have to associate each situation in which the automaton might find itself with the situation it was determined to create. The quasi-mentality of the automaton consists, then, in finding a picture of the instantaneous game situation and bringing about the situation associated with it in the same picture. The surprising property of such an automaton is that given an appropriate repertoire of rules it can—as Turing showed—perform any calculation that a human being might undertake. Of course, a human being has to supply the mentality that is absent by giving the automaton its book of rules. Since the job it has to do is to calculate, the first step in inventing these rules is to decide how numbers will be represented on the tape. Turing chose the so called *unary* representation illustrated below in which a sequence of a certain number of marked cells represents one less than that number (so that 0 too can be represented as a single marked cell). The diagram below shows a tape representing the numbers 0, 1, 2, and 3, separated from one another by unmarked cells.

The automaton now has its own beach of Greek pebbles and its play can begin. To have it calculate 2 + 2, for example, Turing has to supply it with rules that will cause it to transform a tape marked in this way (the automaton is shown in its ready position),

into one marked like this (the automaton is shown ready for its next task.),

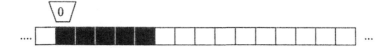

We easily see that the first thing it will have to do is to move to the right until it encounters an unmarked cell which it will then mark.

To this end it will have to be in, let us say, State 1 which is defined by the following pair of rules, the second of which puts it into a second state after it has found and marked the first unmarked cell.

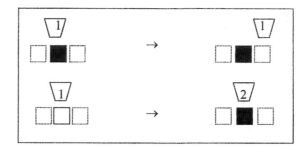

In State 2 it will carry on in the same direction until it encounters another unmarked cell.

When this happens it must change its direction, going into a third state, so that these are the rules defining State 2.

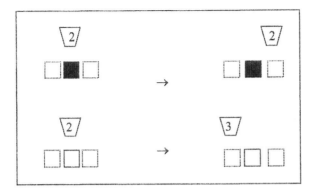

In State 3 the automaton will unmark the two previous cells.

To accomplish this it will have to go through a fourth state and into a fifth. States 3 and 4 are defined by these singleton rules (since the automaton cannot encounter unmarked cells in its first two steps to the left).

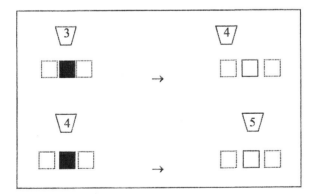

To return to its ready position it must then move to the left in State 5 until it encounters an unmarked cell.

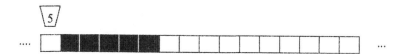

When this happens it will finally move one cell to the right and halt.

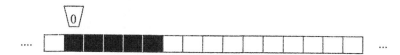

These, then, are the rules by which it plays in this final state.

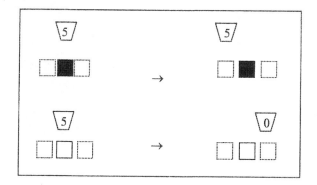

Clearly, the same rules would have the automaton add together any two integers and not just 2 and 2, and equally clearly there is no sense in which following them can be said to constitute the automaton's *understanding* of addition or, indeed, of anything at all. It knows nothing but what is beneath whatever it has for an eye and its own current situation. It can now seem that we have made something rather complicated out of the trivial business of calculating the sum of 2 and 2 but given that these same very simple means can be used to perform any arithmetical calculation, what Turing actually achieves with his automaton is a reduction of the *complexity* of mathematics to the most elemental *simplicity*. It is exclusively his own understanding that is implicit in the rules-matrix he constructs. His work has been massively exploited since his time by the engineers who have realized the automaton he imagined as the computers that now rule the lives of all but the most wary. But Turing's own motivation was that of a mathematician. He wanted to prove that there is no algorism for determining whether equations of certain types have any solution. This he achieved by showing, first, that his automaton can indeed perform any calculation—which, given that the addition operation of elementary arithmetic is the basis of all mathematics, may not surprise us too greatly—and then (by a diagonalization argument in the spirit of Cantor) revealing the subtle contradiction in supposing that it can be known whether the machine will halt in the course of performing a calculation. By imagining this idiot automaton of his—the nadir of simplicity—Turing enables us to *understand* why this—a matter which approaches the zenith of complexity—is as it must be.

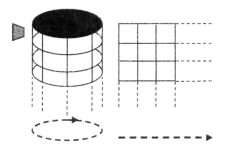

Simulation

54. Turing is hardly suggesting that anything like a ghostly tape is moving past an inner reading- and writing-device inside our heads but rather that his automaton is *simulating* what is going on. What is meant by this is that the automaton—never mind how—is achieving the same result as a human calculator might given the

same problem. The particular interest of cellular automata for our understanding of Science is the use to which they have been put in modelling the complexity of biological processes. To this end Turing's endless tape is replaced by a cylindrical cellular sheet which extends endlessly downwards. Once the sheet has been marked by the automaton it is convenient to slit it open and lay it out flat to examine its surface. The cylinder must be imagined to rotate past the automaton and as it completes each revolution to move upwards so that the automaton can mark the next circle of cells. The automaton is presented with a sheet on which at least some of the cells in the first row have already been marked. What it then does is to mark the second row by following a rule which determines whether a cell is to be marked or left blank on the basis of the markings of, for example, the cell above it and its two neighbours in the same row. There are eight different patterns in which blocks of three cells can be found, *viz.* the following.

The blocks are shown in an order that will seem obvious to a mathematician (that of the binary numerals that they might also represent). Such a rule can be illustrated as in the diagram below.

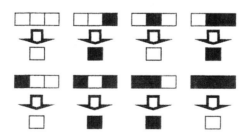

And given that blocks are organized in this determined order it is only necessary to write down the sequence of marked and unmarked blocks in the lower rows to encode the rule completely.

When the behaviour of the automaton is being used to model the emergence of biological complexity this rule is identified with the *genotype* of a living organism. This then is the model strip of DNA corresponding to that genotype.

The model process must be seeded by marking the first row of cells on the cylinder. With one particular choice of seed the automaton generates from this model DNA a marked sheet of which the first few rows are shown below by way of illustration.

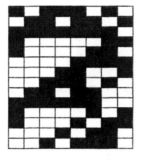

Clearly there is only a finite number of different markings that an entire row can have, in fact just 256 for a sheet like ours with only eight cells to a row. This means that after the automaton has been at work for a while one row pattern must be repeated. There are then exactly two things that can happen: either the same *pattern* or else the same *sequence of patterns* will be repeated endlessly. With other choices of seed-patterns the sheet produced may be very different but it too must eventually arrive at the same repetition or cycle repeatedly through the same sequence. The so-called "Basin of Attraction Field" can now be mapped by

126

plotting each seed and its successive global states as distinct points located on a diagram in accordance with some convention; in this way a picture of the behaviour of the automaton can be obtained. Here we see a picture of it coming to rest at the endless repetition of the same pattern,

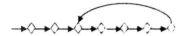

This repeated pattern is the *attractor* towards which the automaton is drawn. In this picture the attractor is a cycle of five repeated states.

A global map of the behaviour of the automaton in which the route towards the attractor from each possible seed is plotted in is the model *phenotype* that develops from the model DNA being studied. When all the arcs are straight lines what emerges is a characteristic picture with a polygonal centre from which depend fans or branches and whilst it can be of very great complexity it will always show a great deal of symmetry (as do the forms generated by the process of life which, in some very general sense, the automaton is intended to model).

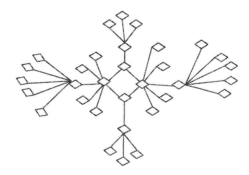

A cellular automaton of this kind also allows the process of genetic mutation to be modelled. In the next drawing we see the effect of such a mutation which is generally to produce a phenotype which is recognizably related to the original but with either more or less complexity. Two mutated genotypes are suggested in the pictures below; the original is shown together with the model DNA with which we began and with two mutated forms which are to be supposed generated by model DNA in which the first and second model genes respectively have been replaced by their converses.

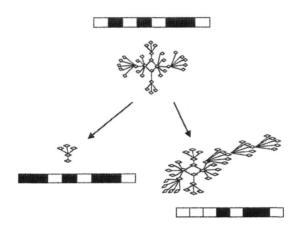

The mating of organisms is similarly modelled by combining the left-half of one DNA-strip with the right half of another. What is found this time (apparently much as in the breeding of animals) is that with similar parents the offspring typically has a mixture of their different characteristics whereas when they are very different it is similar to one of the two.

Summary

55. This chapter has attempted to make the case that the activity peculiar to systematic thinkers is *the construction of models (whether in reality or in*

imagination) that can be manipulated as objects in the world of our experience. The way in which such models supply the semantics for *theoretical terms* was demonstrated by the exhibition of characteristic specimens. The first of these was the mathematical notion of *continuity* for which a model adequate for mathematical purposes is readily available. Doubt was then cast upon the intelligibility of the notion of a *completed discrete infinity*, for which the only model that can be offered fails to satisfy our criterion. The impossibility of making a material model of *Matter* or a spatial model of the *Space* of experience was noted and the *antinomy* of bounded limitlessness was recalled. Models were then exhibited of curved *non-Euclidean spaces* and the evolution of one that is claimed to make intelligible the scientific notion of *Space-Time* was summarily explained. All of these models were then characterized as *static* by comparison with the *dynamic* models that followed. Static models, it was explained, provide the theatre in which the happenings of the world of experience take place; dynamic models are the actors on this stage. Turing's *automated model* of human mentality was presented together with its modification as a *simulation* of the process of Life understood as a system whose evolution is enciphered in a simple code. The scientific value of an adequate model is that explicit *insight* can be drawn from it. It is accordingly to the peculiar scientific form of insight that we next turn our attention.

SYMMETRY

Pattern

56. As the great dictionary of the language makes clear, the word "insight" was originally used with the meaning of *seeing-within-oneself*, but it is its current meaning of *penetrating to what is hidden in whatever it may be one is looking at* that is germane to my present purpose. The systematic thinker examines his representations—the models we have just reviewed—looking for something remarkable to which he can apply his mind. What is remarkable is **pattern**: as we very clearly see when we consider its absence, for what we then have is the randomness on which our minds can get no purchase. A scattering of points, or of straight lines, or of curves would be a picture of randomness precisely to the degree we were unable to find any pattern in it.

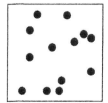 

It was a great challenge faced by the masters of Abstract Impressionist painting to daub their canvasses without any pattern—and, in particular, any likeness of something—emerging from the intended formlessness, but theirs was a deliberately perverse æsthetic. A consideration of what we may know of the culture of our own most primitive ancestors—the universality of body-painting in particular, but also of ornaments and decorations as well as chants and dances, and so on—shows that a delight in pattern must be a very fundamental human trait. But pattern where there should be none can also be disturbing. Thus if we look out of window and down upon the crowd milling about in the central square of the city, what we are likely to see—and indeed what we expect to see—is the sight of as many people moving in any given direction as in any other.

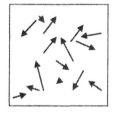 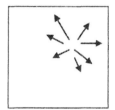

Whilst it prevails such randomness demands no explanation of us but if it should suddenly give way to a pattern, then we look for the reason and find it perhaps in, say, a madman in one corner of the square revealing the bomb concealed within his robe. In finding what it is that made the pattern we have our explanation.

Randomness

57. There is, however, a paradoxical sense in which randomness is also a very special pattern, one to which we are very sensitive. To make a pattern nothing more is needed than a couple of types; ● and O would do as well as any others. Whereas it is a simple matter to arrange tokens of these in a pattern such as this, no doubt the simplest binary pattern of all, ●O●O●O●O●O, it is very difficult

to arrange them without allowing some pattern to emerge, for we see a pattern whenever tokens of one type cluster together, or, rather, whenever this happens we suppose ourselves to see something that is not random. We suppose the same when there are no clusters, as in the example above. Here is a sequence of the same types in which there can seem to be just the right amount of clustering of a single type (there is one cluster of no less than five tokens) and no pattern can be seen:

●O●●O●OO●O●●●●●●O●O●●OOO●●●O●O●OOO●OOO

You might convince yourself that there really is no pattern here by counting the occurrences of O and ● and noting that there are as many of the first as of the second. But that is also true of the very simple pattern I constructed above, so that this cannot be an adequate test of randomness. You might then go on to count the occurrences of the different binary pairs that occur, *viz.* ●●, O●, OO, and ●O and again you would find that all four are equal. On the other hand, such a count would be enough to reveal the lack of randomness of the earlier pattern for there only ●O and O● occur, albeit with equal frequency. You could proceed in this manner by counting the occurrence of the different triplets of these tokens, that is to say ●●●, ●●O, ●O●, ●OO, O●●, O●O, OO●, and OOO; again you will find there to be equally many of all eight. You might now be convinced that this sequence of mine is perfectly random—and you would be quite wrong, for there certainly is a pattern here. I constructed this particular pattern by anticipating the tests you might apply in deciding whether it was a random sequence of the two types. The sequence actually consists of the two singleton types followed by each of the four binary segments and then all eight of the triplet segments (clearly I could go on by adding further longer and longer segments). In the four binary segments taken together, the singletons occur with equal frequency and the same is true of both singletons and binary segments within the segment of triplets. Prediction and randomness seem to go hand in hand: if we could predict

132

the next token in a sequence then we would hardly allow that the sequence was random. No test based upon counting frequencies of occurrences of segments of this kind could reveal a pattern; nevertheless the next member of the sequence can always be predicted, so it cannot be said to be random. There is a paradoxical sense in which absence of pattern is also a pattern.

Normality

58. Closely related to the notion of *randomness i.e.* of the non-existence of pattern in our experience is that of *normal distribution, i.e.* of the particular pattern in which the results of experience cluster around some expectation. This special pattern is demonstrated by an apparatus devised by Galton and accordingly known as the Galton Board. As is shown somewhat schematically in the drawing it is constructed by fixing pegs into a vertical board in such a way that ballots (shown black in the diagram) placed initially on the topmost peg must fall to the left or the right before landing exactly on the centre of a peg in the row below. Its situation is then the same as before and it must continue on its way before landing in one of the containers placed between the gaps in the final row of pegs at the bottom of the board.

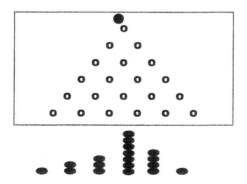

The apparatus is intended to be constructed in such a manner that it could never be predicted to which side a ballot landing on a peg would subsequently fall. This is the justification for saying that the path it actually takes to the bottom of the board where it is collected in a container is, as it were, chosen by the ballot quite at random.

What is interesting, however, is the distribution of the ballots in the containers after a number of trials have been made. This is not a symmetrical distribution in which there are equally many ballots in each. Galton explains the experimental *asymmetry* by indicating an underlying *symmetry* that might escape our notice. All paths through the apparatus are equally long and with the exception of the outermost ones, there are several that would lead a ballot into any given container. These paths can easily be counted and when the totals for the paths to different individual containers are compared with the number of ballots that arrive there (the experiment having been made of sending a sufficient number of ballots through the apparatus), the two are found to be proportionate to one another. When smoothed the totals plotted against the positions of the containers along the bottom edge of the board as a graph make a bell-shaped curve. The function it represents can be expressed analytically which makes it very suitable for mathematical manipulation

It is an easily confirmed observation to arouse the curiosity of the philosopher that the *random* process built into the Galton Board seems to be accepted by both mathematicians and scientists as a suitable model of **normality**. (It is no less curious that mathematicians think of such normality as an empirical fact established by scientists, whereas scientists suppose it to be a properly proven mathematical theorem!) Their shared insight is that in a situation in which experience teaches us that several different outcomes are possible without our having any knowledge of the causal pathways that lead to them we can only have an *expectation* of what the outcome will be supposing each unknown pathway to be followed as often as every other, just as the known pathways are in the situation that Galton contrives with his board. In a situation where this has not been contrived—a situation, that is, that simply occurs in Nature—scientific observers find it to be *normal* that the distribution of outcomes should be very precisely that modelled by the Board and unambiguously *abnormal* that it should not. It seems unworthily *superstitious* that scientists should reject—as they regularly do—any set of observations that are not, in this sense, normally distributed, for it is nothing short of a paradox (one to put alongside the pattern of randomness) that our ignorance should have any structure at all. This is, however, precisely what they do.

Natural Form

59. What we have added to the Dictionary's explanation is that what human insight consists in is the detection of pattern. The general pattern in which we find particular significance is that of *symmetry*. This is the pattern characteristic of all living things and which even the earliest humans strove to make a feature of their artefacts. In particular it is the pattern of our own bodies so that it can be illustrated by considering the human face you shave or paint in the mirror each morning: the two halves of this face are more or less the same. We find a centre-line that divides the face vertically from forehead to chin and along the ridge of the nose. This is an *axis of symmetry* in the sense that every feature—everything that would appear as a point or curve in a drawing of the face—corresponds with another that is the same distance from it at the same horizontal level but on the opposite side: not an eye for an eye, but a right eye for a left one, and so on.

However, no face is quite symmetrical (indeed it seems generally true that nothing in Nature is quite symmetrical, although everything is, as it were, striving to be so); the rare face that is too symmetrical gives an impression of doll-like vacuousness or, perhaps, god-like coldness. Indeed, as the series of drawings below is intended to suggest, portraits contrived by taking the halves of a face and combining each with its mirror image appear to show two different but strangely related individuals.

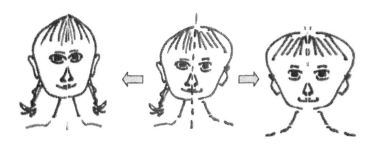

The important point for our understanding of human mentality is that where we find symmetry, we look no further for an explanation: our otherwise relentless search for understanding comes to rest. Where the symmetry of a face is violently broken, we do seek an explanation (which we might find in accident, or disease, or congenital malformation); this too is important: it is **the breach of symmetry** that demands explanation, and we seek it in some other symmetry that is as yet *hidden* from us.

Sufficient Reason

60. Consider what you see when you look at your own reflection in the mirror. It is very familiar but also quite remarkable—at least as soon as we begin to reflect upon it (to make what is not an insignificant pun). The left hand of the man-in-the-mirror (the one upon which he is wearing his watch) is where his right hand ought to be were he a real man standing before you; any hair he might have is parted on the wrong side; that stain on the left edge of your tie is on the right edge of his, and so on: the man-in-the-mirror is transposed about the *longitudinal* axis that runs through his face and down to the floor: the mirror has turned him around. But why is he not also *laterally* transposed: why is his head not where his feet ought to be? To explain this you must locate the hidden asymmetry between the lateral and the longitudinal in the situation which includes you as well as the mirror. To this end you might find yourself considering what would happen were the mirror not on the wall but on the ceiling above your head—and this teaches us

something more about how we work as scientific thinkers: symmetry can of itself be as significant a challenge to our understanding as asymmetry. Thus crystals are very conspicuous objects amongst the generally amorphous stuff of this world; the explanation we seek for their exceptional symmetry is provided by positing a certain structure of matter at a lower, unseen level.

When we find no reason for a difference we are puzzled, as perhaps you were as a child by the child in the mirror; the child destined to be a scientist seeks as its explanation some reason that is sufficient to put its unease to rest. When we look at a balance whose pans are empty, we feel no need to explain why the beam remains horizontal, for the situation is *symmetrical* about the column of the balance. It is when it is not—when, for example, the beam leans to the left—that an explanation is called for. We seek a reason for this broken symmetry and perhaps find sufficient reason in there being something minute but not weightless, something we had not previously noticed (a farthing, perhaps) in the left-hand pan. A reason is sufficient when we feel no need to seek further: once we have uncovered a hidden asymmetry we have our explanation. This is the moral of the story of *Buridan's Ass**. His unfortunate palfrey is to be imagined—and note how I must repeatedly call upon your imagination—locked away for an indefinite period of time in its stable where it is tethered at a point on a line drawn on the floor that precisely divides the space between two quite identical bales of hay. Now, as I retell the story, the animal must starve to death because I have included no reason sufficient for it to choose to begin to nibble either of the bales in preference to the other. If when we go into the stable we find it alive and well, we need an explanation: we need to discover the *hidden asymmetry* (the hidden factor that I have not mentioned, like the little coin in the pan of the balance) that nevertheless made one bale more attractive to it than the other.

If you are inclined to think this an unworthily trivial plea for an unusual conception of understanding then consider this: why is there something in this

---

* Johannes Buridanus was a Fourteenth Century French priest who played an otherwise more or less forgotten minor rôle in the history of logic.

world rather than nothing? Where is the sufficient reason for Nothing becoming just this Reality that we suppose our science to discover—what could be more symmetrical than Nothing, what could contain less hidden asymmetry? We have no answer; we see, indeed, that *there could never be an answer*, because in Nothingness there simply is no asymmetry to point to. (This is, of course, why Religion still has a hold on some otherwise rational people.) As for your mirror image you understand what is happening if you imagine rolling yourself in paint and then pressing your body against the mirror: you see in imagination where your left hand would leave its mark and where your right, and, critically for your understanding, where your head and where your toes would leave theirs. There was only a problem for your understanding if you attended to an *axis of symmetry* that divided the length of your body. What is relevant is the *plane of symmetry* that coincides with the surface of the mirror—and would still have done so had the mirror happened to have been on the ceiling.

Symmetry Operations

61. We understand what is meant by "symmetry" in the case of a face; more generally when we say that something is "symmetrical" we mean that there are things we can imagine ourselves doing with it that would leave its appearance unchanged. This is possible in the case of a symmetrical object because it has sets of parts (*e.g.* the vertices and four sides of a square) that are indistinguishable one from another and so can be permuted without any change in the overall appearance of the object. The investigations of mathematicians begin with some such notion intuitively grasped and proceed by first making it exact and then studying its consequences. There is, then, a strict mathematical use of the term *symmetry* or rather of "**symmetry operation**" in respect of objects of a specific geometrical form. The operations we could perform upon a square object that leave it quite unchanged would be to move it (the operation of *translation*), to turn

it through 90° (*rotation*), and to flip it over about a diagonal or about either of the perpendicular bisectors of its sides (*reflection*).

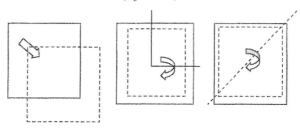

Mathematicians go on to consider the results of combining symmetry operations and to order objects themselves in a hierarchy depending upon how many different operations can be performed upon them that leave them quite unchanged. There are in total eight distinct operations upon the square: the four rotations and four reflections we have considered, in addition, of course, to the countless translations that belong to any physical object. But certain reflections permute the vertices of a square in just the same way as do certain rotations, for example, and whilst something is changed when you catch your reflection in a mirror (a permutation of your hands, and so on), if you find yourself in one of those disorienting places where mirrors are set up at right-angles to one another, then you can catch a reflected reflection of yourself which (albeit uncoloured by the same affection) is just what other people see when they look at you: the watch is back on your right hand where it ought to be.

We have been considering here the symmetry of the *whole* but the simple patterns with which we began this chapter can be seen as the symmetry of *arrangements* of wholes. A pattern we construct consists of a matrix (*i.e.* a structured emptiness ready to receive whatever we might care to put there) in which different elements, ● and O in our examples, are repeated formulaically. The matrix may be linear (as in a frieze) or two-dimensional (as in a carpet or tiled floor), and the symmetry operation in question will be one of translation along a length or breadth or a diagonal.

We are disturbed by any breach of prevailing symmetry, and our characteristic response is to seek an explanation of it: as we have said *asymmetry* always has to be explained. If Buridan's ass survives, our explanation may be that there was something hidden in one of the bales of hay (perhaps some clover, or whatever it is asses particularly like) but not in the other just as in our example of the balance whose pans are apparently empty, we had an explanation for its falling down to one side in discovering in one of its pans a tiny object overlooked before. But we have no explanation of the great metaphysical question, of *why something rather than nothing exists* and, as we have said, we never will, because there could be no asymmetry hidden in primordial nothingness. Neither will we ask questions when the world seems symmetrical enough: the Greeks were satisfied by the impressive central symmetry of the stars and planets wheeling about the earth, on the one hand, and of the linear symmetry of mundane objects left to themselves falling to the ground or rising above it, on the other. Whilst the local *sameness* blinded them to the *difference* in the world as a whole, it was precisely this apparent difference that disquieted Newton and led him to recognize the universal falling together of the material world as a single symmetry that accommodated both spheres.

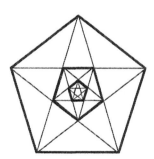

Limitation

62. The *pentagon* has a further symmetry of quite a different kind from the rotations and reflections of the square we considered earlier. When its diagonals are drawn in the resultant *pentagram* is seen to enclose another, smaller pentagon

at its heart; the same is true of the pentagram within this pentagon, and so on, without end. We may say that we understand what is going on in that we can identify an *axiom*—a pentagonal figure—as the *generator* that brings into being a copy of itself at a smaller scale.

axiom   generator

But the vertigo we feel as we look into the inscribed pentagon belies any such claim. We do know how to go on and on towards an end, but that end we do not grasp. The whole that is beyond our human understanding need not be taken for anything more substantial than the limiting artefact of our intellectual exploration of experience. One has some sympathy, however, with those who find in the pentagram the natural emblem of bedevilment. We can construct further examples of infinite iteration by starting with any geometrical figure and inventing a generator that can be applied to it. One such invention is Sierpinski's famous carpet sketched below (to just three levels of complexity) together with its axiom and generator.

axiom   *generator*

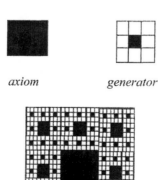

The *self-sameness* of this object—its disturbing property of being exactly the same, no matter how closely we examine it—is, however, a remarkable property of the natural world. We find it, for example, in the shapes of clouds and trees and in the after image of a flash of lightning. We also find it in the coastline of Great Britain or any other island in which every creek and inlet has a similar contour at a smaller scale as the gross outline of a gulf or bay. The Ordinance Survey is a necessary compromise with such intractable infinity as are, of course, all our models of empirical reality. We have only to set ourselves to imagine—as Borges somewhere invites us to do—a map of Great Britain on which a map of Great Britain in all its detail (including then all maps spread out upon it) is shown spread out to be visited by the vertigo of self-referential incomprehensibility.

Invariance

63. A more general notion than the particular sameness of an *individual* thing we have been considering includes the sameness between different particulars. We have identified language as the condition for thought and we recognize now that what is fundamental to it is the symmetry language imposes upon the world by its categorization of things replace one tree with another and (insofar as it is thought of merely as a tree insofar, that is, as it is appropriately schematized) nothing has been changed This notion can, then, be applied to things which have no geometrical symmetry at all.

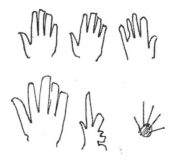

Consider the drawing above of a right hand on a sheet of paper. One symmetry operation would result in an exact copy of it appearing at another place on the same sheet. The second drawing (the transformed object) would then be a *translation* of the first. A translation is a *symmetry operation*, and, for a mathematician, the two drawings constitute a symmetrical pair. Instead of copying the drawing, I might also make a drawing of a left hand of exactly the same size. This drawing would be a *reflection* of the first. In either case a further alternative would be to make the second drawing at either a smaller or a larger scale than the first: such a move is the symmetry operation of *dilation. Translation* leaves the shape, the orientation (or handedness) and the size of the original all unchanged; *reflection* leaves shape and size unchanged, and *dilation* shape alone. (We saw earlier how important dilative symmetry was in the proof of Pythagoras' Theorem.)

For each operation then there is something left *invariant*. But like all mathematical notions that of *symmetry* is only interesting because it makes more precise something vague already familiar in non-mathematical experience. A mathematician might talk of *symmetrical counterparts* intending to be understood in a sophisticated mathematical sense that would include a hand redrawn in a manner that preserved nothing more than certain features of its general structure (this operation might be termed *reduction*). This generalizes the most general notion studied by mathematicians, *viz.* that of *topological invariance*. Its study famously began with the puzzle that apparently filled the leisure of the citizens of Koenigsberg (the once great centre of Prussian learning where Kant took his punctual postprandial promenades). The problem was that of finding a route for a Sunday-afternoon stroll that passed over each and every one of the seven bridges of their city exactly once. Euler (the great Swiss mathematician on his way to St. Petersburg) solved the problem by reducing a map of the city centre to the first graph: a *diagram* rather than a *picture* in which all that remains of the original are nodes where before there were land masses, and edges where before there were the bridges connecting them. Whilst my drawing of the river flowing through the town with its islands and bridges makes no pretention to topographical exactitude, Euler in his austerely topological version eliminates everything but the essential structure of the problem situation: his drawing is the *same* as the original insofar as the problem is concerned. His graph contains everything needed to solve the bridge-crossing conundrum and nothing more; it could conceivably be a similarly useful diagram of quite a different situation which had nothing whatsoever to do with bridges or islands, *e.g.* the underground railway of a small city.

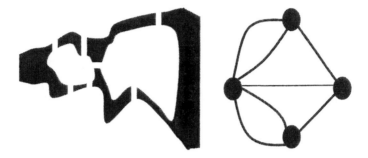

What is obvious to Euler as he considers his graph is that a node that connects *three* edges can only be one of the end points of any circuit which traverses all the edges and that the same is true of one connecting *five* (or indeed any *odd* number) of edges. This informal observation becomes one of the theorems of the developed mathematical theory of graphs and entails, for the application of the diagram that is Euler's problem, that each of the four land masses (the islands and the opposite banks) would have to be one of the two end-points of an appropriate route which is, of course, a condition impossible to fulfil: the dominical perambulation sought by Kant's townsmen does not exist.

But the notion that is useful in understanding Science is even more general than that of topological equivalence. This symmetry is not restricted to geometrical properties (to the contours of figures) but encompasses relations of any intelligible kind. We recall that in analogical reasoning we talk about one

144

thing by talking about another which has the same structure in that the two show themselves to be the same under—as we should now say—some symmetry operation of structural reduction. Things need only be symmetrical counterparts in this very attenuated sense to be the subject of analogical reasoning. The recognition of such symmetry also has the artistic possibilities that, *qua* scientist, are of no interest to the systematic thinker. These are familiar in non-scientific contexts as the metaphor.

Nexus

64. The earliest attempt of which we have any knowledge at a systematic understanding of experience is totemism. The essence of totemic thought as Lévy Bruhl has taught me to understand it[1] is the recognition of a sameness between the jungle and the world within the cave. In ordinary usage we would say that the anthropologist is imputing to primitive thinkers a metaphorical style of thinking in their recognition of a *sympathy between things that are the same,* things that are, then, *symmetrically correlated* one with another (for example, a tribesman on the one hand, and his counterpart—some jungle animal—on the other). In primitive thought the analogical correlation of things—their being symmetrical counterparts of one another—binds them together. There exists between them a **nexus** that seems to be conceived as the conjunction of their fates: whatever happens with the one also happens with the other. Since this can be expected to be so, it would be a catastrophe for a tribesman of the eagle totem if these birds should begin to die out in the forest—but he might damage his enemy, a lion-man, say, by undertaking a campaign of slaughter against the great cats.

The same notion informs another historically important manifestation of pre-scientific thought, *viz. astrology* in which, as we have seen, the nexus in question is between the current condition of the heavens—the location of the wandering planets within the star-pictures of the constellations—on the one hand, and the

---

[1] *q.v.* his *La pensée sauvage.*

tendency of events here on earth, on the other. The existence of such nexus is, in our usual metaphor, a *law* of primitive and pre-scientific thinking, by which is meant a formula compactly summarizing (as has just been done) the application of some intelligible model (the life of animals in the jungle, or the rotation of the heavens, in our examples) to Reality. This is our accustomed way of talking in discussing the results of Science and use of the term *law* should in its turn be recognized as a metaphor—which again suggests how pervasive the use of models may be in all our thinking. But the metaphor is far from being a perfect model, for in human society laws are promulgated and those they are intended to constrain can, albeit at their peril, choose to ignore them. Law is the system in which legal duty and responsibility can be inferred from customs or statutes and has often seemed to be quite literally applied to explanations. We have only to ask whether it is a law of Nature that there are laws of Nature to see how unnatural this part of our theory of Nature really is.

Heuristic

65. Symmetry is something with which we find it particularly easy to deal. A problem which contains no elements of symmetry can be tedious or even difficult to solve. Consider the following problem, some variant of which is traditionally used in making this point. A peasant lives in a hovel and keeps his cow in a shed not too far away. Every morning, he starts the day by going to a nearby beck to fill a pail with water to take to his cow. The problem is to save him unnecessary effort by finding the shortest route he can follow in performing this matutinal task. The problem situation might already be symmetrical, as in the sketch below in which there is an axis normal to the river. In this case we seem to *see* the answer to the problem straight away: there is a certain symmetry in the situation and our intuition—being the human creatures we are with our propensity for symmetry— ought to *respect this symmetry*. The answer is surely that the only path that will do is the one that meets the river half-way between the buildings.

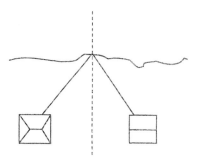

Of course, there is an asymmetry from the *physical* perspective of anybody who knows more about carrying buckets of water than philosophers typically do, because, once filled, the bucket is much heavier than before; we, however, concentrate upon the purely geometrical problem. But is this the right answer? How do we *see* that any other path must be longer? The shortest path between two points is the straight line that joins them; in what sense is this crooked path a *straight* line?—Well, to see that we must first **impose more symmetry** by embedding the problem situation (the hovel, the shed and the stream) in a wider situation in which a ghost hovel and a ghost shed have been introduced on the other side of the beck so that it has become a second axis of a reflection.

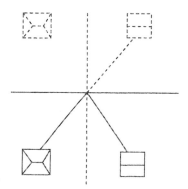

How does this help?—Well, it is clear *from the symmetry* of the object consisting of the four buildings and the brook that the ghost path between buildings to or from any spot at the water's edge is exactly as long as the corresponding real path. And, more significantly, any path that crosses the beck (now supposed to be very narrow) in going from the real hovel to the ghost shed is just as long as one that meets the beck at the same spot and then turns away to go to the real shed. It was by somehow exploiting this symmetry that we "saw" which path was shortest, for the shortest path from the hovel to the ghost shed crosses the beck at the same spot as it is touched by the shortest route from the hovel to the real shed—*i.e.* the straight line between hovel and ghost-shed shows the peasant the spot at which to fill his bucket.

Insight

66. Of course our peasant could have solved the problem for himself by an undemanding exercise in the calculus of variations (this is an elementary extremum-problem); that, however, would have given him an answer to his particular problem but no *insight* whatsoever. By contrast an **insight** into many other problems is precisely what we have gained from having seen this wider symmetry. This is what it is to solve a problem: we structure and then restructure what we are given until we *see* the sameness originally concealed within it. Insight is just this seeing in a fresh way. In a complicated situation in which hovel and shed are not symmetrically arranged with respect to the river we would not before having reasoned in this way have seen which of the many possible paths shown below is the shortest.

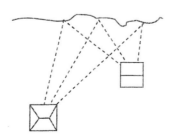

But now we do so, and that immediately! Our insight has, as it were, been *educated* by the little piece of reasoning I have just shown you. We will from now on see the solution to any problem with a similar manifest structure. You—but not the man who had *calculated* the right answer—now *see* all such situations in this light:

You may find, as I do, that there is something powerful and elegant about this demonstration (which dates back, as does so much that is powerful and elegant to the ancient Greeks, at least to the *Catoptrica* of Hero of Alexandria). Science values the use of symbols very highly, so it is salutary to observe how **non-symbolic** this piece of reasoning is: whilst I did, of course, need to use words like *hovel*, *beck* and *shed* to set up the problem, it was solved by drawing pictures (*i.e.* by making a *model* of the problematic situation). You looked at my drawing and something remarkable happened: you were—as I suggested—*possessed* of a certain insight. It is such possession that constitutes understanding. It seems hardly possible to say anything more about this state than that when we are so possessed we rest satisfied. It came in this case as I think it very often does from exploring the symmetry peculiar to an individual problem.

This particular insight now becomes a problem-solving tool that we take with us and find use for in situations which *on the surface* are quite unrelated. The ellipse, for example, is (as we shall see) a geometrical figure of great importance in the history of science. Children are shown how to draw it by looping a string around two pins stuck through a piece of paper on a table, inserting a pencil into the loop and allowing it to trace out a contour as the string is kept taught: the ellipse is, in other words, the locus of points the sum of whose distances from two fixed points is constant. The points pierced by the pins are the two foci of the ellipse.

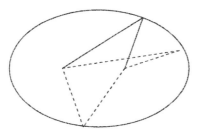

The shortest path between the foci visiting a point on the circumference on the way—and the mere mention of "the shortest path" brings our thoughts back to the peasant's problem with his bucket of water—is the same for any such point: it consists of following first the straight line to the point from either focus and then the straight line back to the other focus. Now consider the tangent to the point on the circumference visited on such a journey. Because this path is the shortest, my drawing of the ellipse with its tangent and foci has the same symmetry as the field with its brook, hovel and shed. There is a sense in which my picture of the one is the same as my drawing of the other. This is immediately clear when the two are displayed alongside one another as they are below.

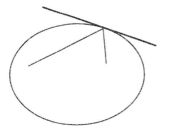
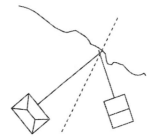

Having educated our intuition as we have by a study of the peasant's problem, we now *see* that were the straight line from either focus to be continued beyond the ellipse, (as both are by dotted segments in the next drawing), it would arrive at a ghost point which would be the reflection in the tangent of the other focus.

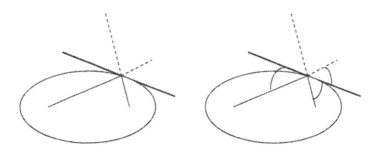

By very simple considerations of the further symmetry of the drawing we also see that the three angles marked in my drawing are equal so that we know something that can be enunciated in this geometrical *law: any tangent to an ellipse makes equal angles with its radii at the point of tangency.* Now, our first drawing of the ellipse might have been the scientist's *model* of the orbit of a satellite about its planet. What would then have been demonstrated above would be the uncovering of something latent in the model or what we have described as the extraction of *insight* from it. What was found was a pattern already familiar to us—that of the symmetrical scene of our rural digression above. It is the argument of the present essay that such a movement is the essential characteristic of scientific thought and a repertoire of patterns to be sought the scientist's essential tool.

Particularity

67. The abstruseness of the knowledge applied is a further indication of the power of thinking in terms of symmetry—but also of its limitations. There is no standard method (such as the calculus which could also have been applied in this situation) for discovering the latent symmetry of a problem and each new insight is *sui*

generis. The totally unrelated symmetry of another problem will underline this point. Consider a floor that might be covered by square tiles arranged within a four-by-four matrix. We easily see that it might also be covered by rectangular tiles each the size of two of these square tiles placed side by side.

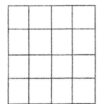 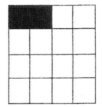

But what of the similar tessellation of an area which was as before except that two diametrically opposite squares were not to be covered. We can hardly *see* immediately whether the rectangular tiles could be used in this case. But we can imaginatively restructure the floor and impose a symmetry upon it that enables us to do just that. The symmetry in question is the chequered pattern of a chessboard in which neighbouring squares in either direction are of opposite colours.

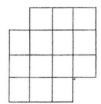 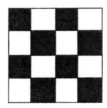

Having imposed this symmetry we see that in covering the unmutilated matrix with our rectangular tiles, no matter how we might choose to do this, each tile must cover one black square and one white one. A tiling of the mutilated floor would have to fulfil the same condition, but we see that it could not do so because the squares that have been excised from the board are of the same colour which

152

entails that there are now more white squares than black ones. In the terminology of the present discussion the two diagrams above are a *model* of the floor and the *pattern* that would have to be found present within it were the tessellation to succeed. Again our intuition has been educated; it is, perhaps, not inconceivable that another problem situation having the same hidden symmetry as this may one day come along.

Atomic Structure

68. Modern chemistry begins with the careful weighing of the elementary constituents of compound substances. This enables the relative weight of each element to be determined and the composition of their compounds to be assigned an *empirical formula*. Thus the formula of alcohol is found to be C_2H_6O, in which the elemental substances in question are identified by symbols (C, H, and O), typically the initials of their common English or Latin names (Carbon, Hydrogen, and Oxygen), and the relative number of units of each is denoted by a subscript appended to its symbol (so that, in the case of alcohol, there are two units of carbon and six of hydrogen for each unit of oxygen). The chemist can generally induce elementary substances to combine with hydrogen and he then declares the element to have a *valency* which is the number of units of hydrogen which are found to be required. What chemists also find is that several substances can have one and the same empirical formula. Thus Ether, for example, has the same constitution as Alcohol, and that despite their chemical (not to say biological) properties being very different. There is then some hidden asymmetry that somehow underlies this empirical similarity.

What insight can be gained into this asymmetry?—For the chemist to grasp it he must produce a *representation* of some hidden structure manifest in the qualitative difference. This he assembles on the basis of tokens of the letters abbreviating the names of elements each furnished with a number of strokes emanating from it to correspond to its valency. The general element of his model is thus of this from.

He arranges his tokens on the picture surface—the requisite number of each being extracted from the empirical formula—and connects them one to another by amalgamating one stroke belonging to each of two tokens as a single stroke.

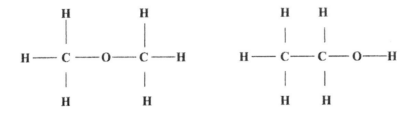

He finds that he can produce at least two quite different representations of the formula C_2H_6O, *viz.* those shown here. These are the *structural formulæ* now identified with Ether and Alcohol, respectively; what is manifest in the possibility of constructing these different diagrams is now co-ordinated by the chemist with the hidden difference that accounts for the empirical asymmetry: these are representations of the compounds that can, then, show their hidden natures. The existence of atoms is an ancient Greek idea but the recognition that these structural formulæ reveal something empirically real brings into being the precise chemical notions of an *atom* of an element and of a *molecule* of a chemical compound: a molecule comes to be the spatial arrangement of a bonded collection of atoms. The chemist's *model* in all this is the empirical formula—not, however, considered as the token of a symbolic type but as a material object whose parts are rather like the letter-blocks with which pre-school children are sometimes encouraged to play. *Insight* consists in the discovery of a pattern of arrangement of these parts that respects the laws of valency.

Evolution

69. The chemist sets himself to discover the structure hidden within matter. Modern Biology begins with the attempt to describe the structure in which living things have their places—a structure that is not obviously hidden from view by the grossness of our senses but rather by the overwhelming abundance of forms of life. Natural language supplies us with the names of classes of animals, "ape," "fish," "worm," "pig," and so on which are far too vague for the purposes of the naturalist and *unsystematic* in that they do not of themselves reveal anything about the relationships of the animals they designate. The Swedish botanist Carl von Linné showed in his famous *Systema Naturæ* how this diversity might be reduced to order by the device of arranging species within a hierarchy of taxa. The basis of his taxonomical arrangement is the intimate details of the anatomical structure of plants and animals. Our familiarity with this procedure should not hide the brilliance of Linnæus' selection of it, for it is very far from being determined in any way by the unclassified material. This is very clear when one recalls the differentia by which Aristotle specifies the essence of humanity: we are the *bipeds*, he tells us, which are both *featherless* and *rational*; the apes are *tree-living* bipeds.

When completed a diagram of this arrangement shows the continuously branching system of the root of a tree. At its apex is the taxon which includes all species of living things. and each of the terminals is labelled with the Linnæan name of one of the species found by naturalists in their exploration of the world. The branching serves, first, to gather close together those whose structures are similar (such as chimpanzees, gorillas and baboons) whilst keeping widely apart those whose structures are not (such as chimpanzees, jellyfish and buttercups) and, secondly, to supply *systematic names* for them all, names, that is, which reflect precisely a place in the system by naming in turn the sequence of branches (each of which is named) by which it is reached starting from the apex. The other great virtue of the system is that it can readily be expanded or modified (by moving branches) to provide a place for any new species discovered by intrepid explorers of the deep ocean or of what is left of the rain-forest. The diagram below is a schematic representation of a hieroglyphic version of the whole which will serve my present purposes without having any pretension to biological plausibility. No attempt is made here at even suggesting the systematicity of naming that is the *raison d'être* of the Linné's original.

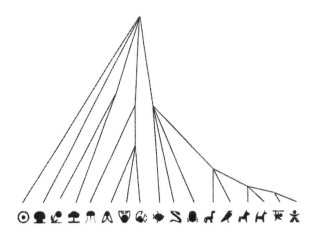

The immediate purpose of its author in constructing this system may have been nothing more than to unify the study of Nature by unambiguously naming species and providing the means of re-identifying them (by attaching to each name a list of anatomical characteristics) but the effect of a representation of the system was, for the first time, to bring the living world into being for us as one whole.

Brought up to date by the successors of its first author a diagram of this system is our *model* of the living world. As has been repeatedly stressed a representation of this sort is the essential prerequisite for the attainment of insight but no picture of any kind can of itself tell us how it is to be seen or determine what will be found in it. What Darwin and Wallace had to do before the Theory of Evolution could set Nature Study on the road to biological science was to find the pattern hidden in this diagram. This only becomes apparent when it is reinterpreted and seen not as the *synchronic* representation of the living world intended by Linnæus himself (*i.e.* as one that shows what organisms are to be found alive today) but as a *diachronic* one that shows how their diversity arose. Darwin and Wallace taught us to see the living world that Linnæus brought into being as itself something that had grown in anatomical complexity from a primitive beginning. They saw the diagram of his system as itself a living organism, as a *tree*.

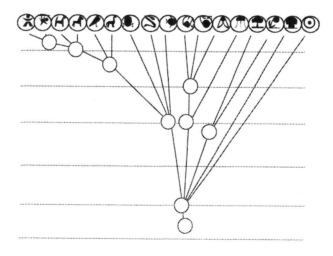

Trees are mathematical as well as biological objects; in mathematical guise they are closely related to Euler's graphs but the edges of the diagrams are directed, rather like arrows; the trunk at the bottom leads up to branches which lead ultimately to leaves at the top. These *leaves* are the extant forms that life has taken, whilst the *nodes* from which new branches issue are the ancestral organisms of all those found on those branches. Only the fossilized remains of these are ever found but the geological formations in which they occur enable their relative ages to be ascertained. The root-system of the Linnæen model can be turned on its head and superimposed upon a representation of geological strata to become the picture of the evolution of the living world. The structure hidden within it is that of genetic *descent*, so that the tree shows the *ascent* from primæval simplicity of the complex forms of life we see about us today.

Genetic Structure

70. An entirely separate insight is needed to arrive at an understanding of how forms of life could evolve at all. That insight occurred to a monastery-gardener and reluctant abbot who figures in history, somewhat romantically, as the solitary father of the now burgeoning science of Genetics. To grasp the insight for which Mendel is famous the non-gardener must know that a peculiarity of the pea-plant is that whilst it can be cross-fertilized it will, should this not occur, fertilize itself. He must also know that the peas these plants produce are either rounded or wrinkled and angular (in addition to many other varying characteristics they may have). Mendel's fundamental observation was that when rounded-pea producing plants which are pure-bred in the sense that they descend from generations of plants with the same characteristic are artificially cross-fertilized with similarly pure-bred angular-pea producing plants their offspring always produce rounded peas. The charts of a human genealogist (such as that of the incestuous inhabitants of Elsinore) suggest an appropriate model.

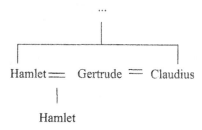

The drawings below set out the genetic peculiarities of the peas explained above in the same fashion (plants being represented by the shapes of their peas).

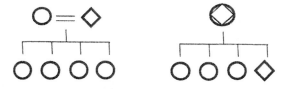

Mendel describes this model by saying that roundness in the pea is a *dominant* hereditary characteristic. However, the hybrid plants are not the same as their pure-bred progenitors. They are represented in the second diagram by a symbol which combines the rounded and angular ones from the first and what is suggested is that when the hybrids are allowed to fertilize themselves a strange *asymmetry* is observed in their offspring: only three out of every four of them possess this dominant characteristic. Mendel seeks out the symmetry that must lie somewhere behind such an oddly asymmetric result and he finds what will serve his purpose in postulating hidden *factors of heredity* as part of the constitution of all individual plants. The factor that is inherited by an angular-pea producing plant must somehow be latent in the hybrid despite its own production of rounded peas. As Mendel expresses this, angularity in the pea is a *recessive* hereditary characteristic.

A scheme that has the desired symmetry and produces the empirically observed result is suggested in the diagram below in which both the external appearance of plants and their hidden hereditary structure are shown in each case. As indicated the gametes of each plant must be supposed to contain two factors like coins in a purse; each offspring inherits one factor from each parent plant, so that there are four ways in which this can be done. The inheritance of the offspring is the same in every case, so that all are hybrid plants producing rounded peas but containing both factors.

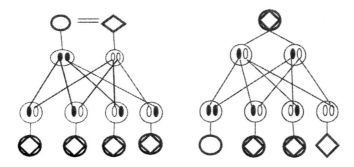

However, when hybrid plants are self-fertilized the four ways in which the offspring can inherit their two factors no longer have the same result, for each gamete contains both factors. Mendel knew no more than we do of anything that might determine which of these ways would be implicated in any particular case. In finding their way to expression, his factors were then, for all Mendel could know, in the same state of balance as ballots on the pegs of Galton's board, so that all four ways had equal chances of being followed. One of these ways results in a plant with angular peas, one which will in future breed true; of the other three ways one produces a pure-bred round pea plant and the other two hybrids. There are thus three times as many of the one variety as of the other in accordance with empirical results obtained in the monastery garden. It is not just Mendel's search for hidden symmetry that is of interest here but also his recognition of the equal *probability* of each combination of inherited factors. Why are they equally probable?—Well, in his complete ignorance of the mechanism of biological inheritance Mendel knew of no reason why any should be preferred over others. Mendel's *model* in all this is the pair of genealogical diagrams with the three different symbols that are needed to distinguish their genetic characters. His great *insight* is contained in the embellishment of this model with representations of the purses of hereditary factors which interrupt the lines of descent and reveal the hidden structure which is the explanation of this genetic difference.

Decryption

71. At the beginning of this essay *syntax* was explained as the organizing pattern manifest in the sentences of a language. It will be recalled that in the syntax of out hieroglyphic model a very simple sentence such as ▰ ⚘ 大, consisted of tokens selected from the types which constitute the categorized vocabulary of the language arranged in the sequence exemplified by this sentence. Given this syntactical rule any change of the sequence, *e.g.* to 大 ⚘ ▰, would result in a sentence with quite a different *meaning*. It was explained that a claim of this hieroglyphic language to be a model of human language would depend upon exhibiting the rules by which meaningful English sentences were *encoded* in the hieroglyphic symbols.

The microscopic examination of the tissue of living things reveals them to be built up of cells. The chemical machinery by which cells replicate and multiply has been extensively studied and, in particular, the implication in this process of the very large molecules of a substance known to the biochemist—and, indeed, the general population—as *DNA* has been uncovered. When this molecule is unwound from the spiral structure in which it occurs and dissociated from the twin to which it is bound in the nucleus of the cell it is found to consist of a long chain in which certain very much smaller molecules, usually termed *bases*, are concatenated. These are tokens of just four types repeated in a long sequence in which no pattern is discernable so that its complexity approaches that of randomness. This pattern brings to mind a line of text in a book. The molecule might then be represented in this manner:

The Greeks wrote their books in lines of unpunctuated majuscules. In our editions, as a first step to grasping the meaning, we punctuate these lines with gaps and so isolate individual words. The molecular biologist does much the same for he finds that the secret to interpretation is the imposition of a *pattern* that makes each words a sequence of just three letters:

... ♥♣♦ ♥♦♥ ♣♥♦ ♣♦♦ ♣♣♥ ... .

Each three-letter word is a so-called *codon* and, in being a word, each has its own *meaning* which in each case is one of the amino acids that the cell can manufacture. Any sequence of codons has as its meaning one of the larger molecules known as *proteins* made out of these acids and themselves the stuff of the tissue of living things.

Mendel's "factors of inheritance" have become the "genes" of Molecular Biology; each of these is a portion (a sentence, as it were) of the molecular strand. In the hieroglyphic model the words are iconic representations of their meanings but no such simple relationship exists between a strand of DNA and the organism to which it belongs; indeed, nothing at all seems to be known about this relationship. History advises caution but one suspects that nothing ever will; certainly a completely different approach to the whole of Science will be needed to unify chemistry (with its roots in quantum mechanics) and morphology (with its roots in human perception), to understand how, for example, an individual human being is, as we say, *encoded in his genes*. Nevertheless, the understanding of the chemical machinery of the cell is a momentous achievement and when the replication of generations of cells is viewed as analogous to the party game in which a message is passed around a room to arrive back where it began in unrecognizable form something very important about biological inheritance, about Mendel's peas and Darwin's Tree of Life, seems to become comprehensible.

There is nothing mysterious about the *mutation* of the message as it passes between the lips of one excited whisperer and the ears of the next against a background of noisy revelry. Mutation is the key to understanding inheritance with variation and the garbling of an incoherent message to understanding monstrosity or congenital disease. A string of letters is our modern model of Mendel's purse of genetic factors and the insight that makes it possible to describe in great detail the chemical activity of the cell is the recognition of a syntactical pattern and the semantics of the words organized by it.

Algorism

72. The oldest mathematical texts that survive are apparently certain clay tablets inscribed in cuneiform script. The translations show them to be demonstrations of the application of arithmetical techniques. Their purpose is clearly to provide paradigms for the solution of standard problems, so that each ends appropriately with the phrase "Such is the way to proceed." Euclid's texts by way of significant contrast complete their conclusions with the phrase (in the familiar Latin version), "quod erat demonstrandum," *i.e.* "which is what was to be proved." In the arithmetical part of his "Elements," Euclid provides a famous algorism for calculating the *highest common factor* of two given integral numbers.

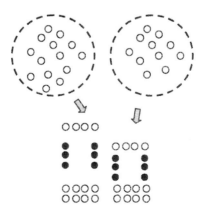

What this means in terms of the Greek games with collections of pebbles is illustrated in the accompanying diagram: the collections shown have to be arranged as rectangular numbers erected on the same base (which is 4 in the drawing for the sake of definiteness); whenever this can be done the base is a common factor and the largest such base is the number sought. Had Euclid done his work in Babylonian style he might have chosen the calculation of the highest common factor of, say, 112 and 21. He would have instructed his reader to subtract the smaller from the larger to arrive at 91, and then to go on in similar fashion. Taking 21 from 91 the reader would obtain 70; taking 21 from 70, 49; taking 21 from 49, 28; and finally taking 21 from 28, 7 which is indeed the *hcf* (as mathematicians are wont to write) of the original numbers. Now the reader knows the way to proceed (although another couple of examples would be useful to let him know how to go on when certain complications arise), but what has he *understood*? I think we may agree that he need hardly have understood more than an Egyptian foreman-builder with twelve cubits of knotted rope.

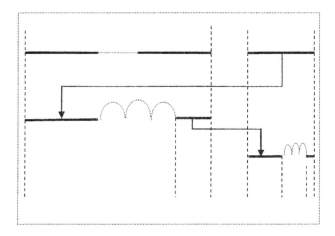

Euclid, of course, describes the procedure in complete generality and supplies a proof that when the end is reached the number obtained really is the highest common factor. He starts as we expect with a diagram which I have attempted to make more intelligible in the version immediately above. He represents the two integers as lines whose lengths are proportionate to them, the larger to the left and the smaller to the right at the top of my diagram. (The diagram shows only the first two iterations of the algorism whereas many more might be required; I have inserted a conventional row of dots in the middle of the first line to indicate that it is indefinitely longer than the second and have not even tried to keep things in proportion.) What has to be done is to try to measure—in a technical sense that will become clear—the longer of the two lines at the top with the shorter. If one could measure it in the intended sense, there would be no remainder left over and the smaller number itself would obviously be the *hcf* of the pair (in the diagram what you see below the longer line is the shorter one followed by bows intended to suggest an indefinite number of iterations of it). If, however, there is a remainder (as there is in the diagram, *viz.* the line segment following the bows) and this remainder is just one unit of measurement, then the given numbers are *relatively prime* in that they can have no common factors. In the more general case, however, there will be a non-unit remainder which must now be carefully considered.

What has to be grasped—and this is the only point of difficulty—is that the *hcf* of the original numbers is also that of the smaller number and whichever number may now be represented by the remainder. This is seen to be so because to *measure* (in Euclid's technical sense) the longer line is the same as to *measure* the shorter (however many times it may have been iterated) and to *measure* the remainder. This is the crucial insight that the rote learning of practical rules is unlikely ever to instil. What now has to be found is the *hcf* of the smaller of the given numbers and this remainder, so that the way to proceed is to do with these two lengths exactly the same as was done with those at the top of the diagram, and so on until two lengths which are the same are obtained when the whole business must come to a halt. Observe how I have struggled to say all this in words (and perhaps you have struggled to follow) but also how easy it all becomes once the Euclidean drawing has been properly interpreted. This insight is clearly something altogether different from merely working the algorism; on the other hand, to have invented the recursive process is certainly to have a profound insight into an aspect of the structure of the system of natural numbers.

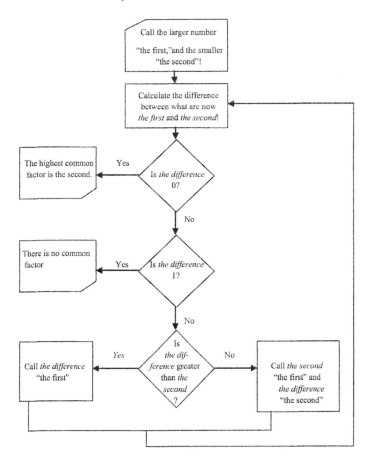

Once attained—but only then—this insight can be incorporated into one of the so-called "flow-diagrams" that are used particularly by the people who programme computing machines. The diagram shown here might be the first move in writing a programme that would make such a machine (which is, of course, irredeemably

Babylonian in having no understanding of what it is doing) follow Euclid's algorism. Such diagrams observe a variety of conventions: in mine I have used boxes of different shapes to represent what is put into the machine, the simple operations to be performed by it, and what it puts out before it comes to a halt and I have used lozenges to represent the decisions that have to be taken. All of these are filled with sentences of natural language.

However it may be constructed, the rôle of such a flow-diagram in the programmer's thought is important for an understanding of the process we call scientific thinking and we shall return to it in our final chapter. What I want to stress now, however, is that the flow-diagram is an *intermediary* between the intuitive representation of Euclid's geometrical diagram and his text. A more direct translation of the flow-diagram into our modern idiom (influenced as it is by the business of writing programmes for our idiot computers) would be the following.

Do this repeatedly:

> *Calculate the difference between the two numbers.*
>
> *If the difference is 0, conclude that the highest common factor is the smaller number.*
>
> *If the difference is1, conclude that there is no common factor.*
>
> *If the difference is greater than the smaller number, then let it replace the first number.*
>
> *If the difference is less than the smaller number, then let the second number replace the first and the difference replace the second number.*

We perform simple calculations—including perhaps finding the highest common factor of 112 and 21—without seeing how we do it. But in even slightly more challenging cases we need something very like this version of Euclid's algorism. Given the numbers 12378 and 3054, for example, we are lost unless we can blindly follow the step-by-step instructions written out here and find that the first and second numbers take on these successive pairs of values: 9323, 6108; 6108, 3216; 3216, 3054; 3054, 162; 162, 138; 138, 24; 24, 18; 18, 6; 6, 6. Given the confidence it deserves in this two-thousand year old algorism, we blighthly conclude that their highest common factor is 6.

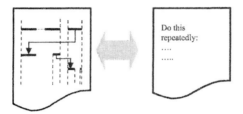

We know what we are doing only to the degree we can give expression to it. This algorismic procedure begins, then, with the *intuition* of how some calculation is done, or might be done. Euclid gave his intuition expression in what it accordingly seems appropriate to call an *intuitive model*, *viz*. his drawing of line segments. The end of the process was a text which must be seen as a symbolic analogy of the intuitive model. In fact the intuitive model provides the *semantics* for this *syntactical* object. But between the two—and as a bridge between them—there is room for something else, *viz*. a hybrid or, better, a Janus-faced thing in which linguistic elements (descriptions, that is, of stages in the modelled process) are geometrically organized. Such an intermediary is a ***syntactico-semantic*** entity that seems to be the locus of our understanding of Euclid's algorism. On the one hand, the original drawing is in want of explanation because, as we have often observed, no picture can tell us how it is intended to be *seen*; on the other hand, the programmatic text is something for us to follow as blindly as a Babylonian clerk or Turing's automaton (and as you perhaps just did). It is this relationship that I have tried to suggest in the last drawing.

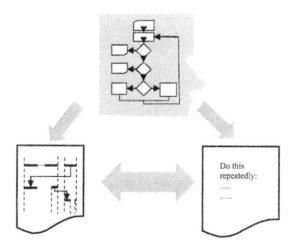

There is, the gods being merciful, no flow-diagram to accompany Euclid's text and certainly no part of it reads at all like a computer programme; what he gives us is a geometrical drawing and a text that tells how to interpret it, supplying at the same time the argument that justifies his claim that his procedure determines a highest common factor. What my flow-diagram does is to extract from his text the simple procedural elements that are implied and arrange them, step by step, in a single branching sequence. As my drawing is intended to suggest the flow-diagram is a model of what Euclid must seem to have *had in mind* as he wrote out his text. It gives expression to the *insight* derived from the geometrical drawing that is his *model* of the original game played with pebbles on a Greek beach. What is seen in this inner way is, as always, a pattern; on this occasion the pattern is the special form of symmetry we call recursion but one that unlike Sierpinski's Carpet comes to a satisfactory end.

Summary

73. The previous chapter was designed to suggest the ubiquitousness in scientific work of the real or imaginary construction of *material models* of a particular kind. In the present chapter we have examined the notion of scientific insight and found it to be the discovery of *pattern* in the models we construct. The paradox that *randomness* is itself a singular pattern was noted as was the no less paradoxical recognition of *normal distribution* as the invariable pattern of scientific ignorance. We recalled the pervasiveness of *symmetry* in the products of Nature and suggested that a *breach of symmetry* is the typical occasion of the search for an explanation identifying some *sufficient reason* for the breach. The mathematical notion of symmetry was explained and its heuristic value demonstrated as was the manner in which *insight is educated by problem-solving*. The important concomitant notion of *structural invariance* was introduced and examples presented of the way in which scientific understanding is the uncovering of *latent structure* in the world of experience. These examples were chosen to underline the centrality of the procedure in Chemistry and the life-sciences. The notion of a pattern's carrying *encrypted information* was also explored and, finally, the concept of *algorism* demonstrated and explained as the imposition of a pattern of recursion in an operational procedure.

The chapter that follows (and is largely continuous with the present discussion) will attempt to explain the relationship between the patterns uncovered in the examination of a model and the symbolic system by means of which it is exploited.

SYMBOLIZATION

Calculation

74. Euclid's proof of the Pythagorean Theorem contains a purely verbal argument which we find to conform to our logical expectations. One recalls Clausewitz' famous remark that war is just diplomacy carried on by other means—means which we know to be far more persuasive. In the scientist's striving to attain understanding, mathematics is the persuasive means by which argument is carried on after words alone give out. In arguing with mathematics we rely upon symbols. But *symbolism* (by which I mean the adoption of symbols beyond the letters with which we write down words) is not a natural affair. The collections of pebbles on the beach with which I have shown you the Greeks playing their counting games are models of numbers but these models are not symbolic things in the sense I am trying to clarify. They are, rather, *intuitive models* in that they seem to appeal directly to intuition without the mediation of symbols. The distinction I want to make is clear when what the Greeks called the ἀβαξ (whence our "abacus") is considered.

We humans cannot immediately see how many pebbles there are in a heap unless the number is one, two, three or four. If there are no more than just five we have to count them to know how many are there. One can imagine that the abacus evolved from a refinement of the Counting–Game in which lines were drawn in the sand and pebbles arranged along them to make it possible to *read* a total without having to count every pebble. The essential move is tedious to put into words but is easily grasped from a drawing of the most primitive abacus one can imagine.

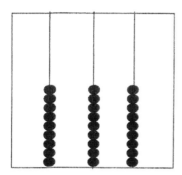 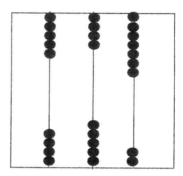

Instead of pebbles along grooves in the sand, beads move on wires suspended within a frame; there are nine beads (which stay where they are when not being moved) on each wire and the game starts with all of them at the bottom of the frame. As things are counted beads on the rightmost wire are moved to the top of the frame. When there are no beads left to move on a given wire, all nine are put back to the bottom and one bead moved up on the next wire to the left. In this manner 547 things would have been counted when the apparatus is in the state shown in the drawing to the right above. *Subitation* is the human faculty for taking something in all at once in a single glance. We could not, of course see in this way that there were 547 beads in a pile on the table, but, knowing as we now do the rules for playing the abacus game, we easily *see* that the beads have been moved 547 times from the starting position—and we would do so by subitation had there been no more than five beads in any group. The fully developed abacus (which apparently still survives in our age of miniaturized electronic devices as the *suan pan* in China) has only five beads on a wire and a transverse beam separating the topmost from the others.

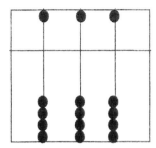 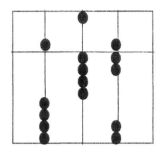

The start position is shown here to the left and the manner of operation is evident once one knows that the apparatus to the right allows its operator to see that again 547 things have been counted. The reason I do not want to say that this *drawing* is a *symbol* is that it cannot be manipulated in the Clausewitzian continuation of argument.

Mathematical symbols can, but they can also be more or less well–suited to the task for which we employ them as is immediately apparent when we consider what would be involved in obtaining even the simplest arithmetical results by using Roman numerals. The numerals of all familiar natural languages, including, of course, Latin, are perfectly adequate in that given any one of them, one can immediately write down the next. The same is true of the Roman symbols for their numerals, *I* for *unus*, *V* for *quinque*, *X* for *decem*, and so on, when these are combined with the positional rules for successors and predecessors in the sequence which generate *II* for *duo* and *VI* for *sex*, *IV* for *quattuor* and *IX* for *novem*, and so on (these choices have nothing to do with the spellings of the Latin numerals but do vaguely suggest the operations of the abacus). The way in which this is done in natural languages—by the recursive use of the same sounds—is as astonishing as so much is in the structure of language, but consideration of it serves to remind us that the use of mathematical symbols is an extension of our use of natural language and not something of a different kind. The historical evolution of the most elementary modern arithmetical sentence seems to have been somewhat on the following lines:

Quinque plus septem est duodecim;

v plus vii est xii

v p vii ε xii;

5 p 7 ε 12.

5 + 7 = 12.

We see from this that the arithmetical sentence is a sentence of language incorporating certain abbreviations for natural words. The characteristic constituent of peculiarly mathematical sentences is the abbreviation for "equals," "="; such a mathematical sentence is an *equation*. The superiority of the modern symbols which have enabled Science to evolve lies in this: the *rules* of the game played with Arabic numerals are easily written down in the form of addition and multiplication tables involving only the primitive recursive elements (the numerals from 0 to 9) whereas there are no corresponding rules for their Roman predecessors. The letters *I, V, X, L, C, D* and *M,* are nothing more nor less than abbreviations for Latin words and the real calculating is done by, for example, saying these words as one counts on one's fingers or the beads of an abacus.

It is instructive to observe the way in which we *carry on arguing* with mathematical symbols in the most trivial cases. Here is the pedantically detailed protocol of a typical example.

There are five apples on this tree and seven on that one.

5 is the number of apples on one tree, 7 the number of apples on the other.

5 + 7 = 12

12 is the total of these numbers, so there are twelve apples on these trees.

What we observe is this: that a statement made in natural language is reformulated by substituting symbols (here "5" and "7") for certain of its words. These symbols are then concatenated observing the rules of syntax peculiar to the mathematical extension of language to produce a mathematical formula ("5 + 7"). This formula is written down and a mathematical sentence composed by appending the symbol "=" and writing down a new phrase (here the symbol "12") to its right. A word of natural language ("twelve") is then substituted for this phrase and a new statement composed. It is the process of composing the mathematical sentence containing the sign "=" that we call *calculation*. It consists of translating what is first said in words into symbols of a distinctive kind and manipulating these symbols before translating them back into words.

V

+	1	2	3	4	5	6	7	...
1	2	3	4	5	6	7	8	...
2	3	4	5	6	7	8	9	...
3	4	5	6	7	8	9	10	...
4	5	6	7	8	9	10	11	...
5	6	7	8	9	10	11	12	...
...	...	...	...	...	...	...	...	...

(">" marker to the left of the "5" row)

How was this calculation performed? —Well, what was done in this case might have been done by consulting some version of the familiar addition table shown here. For to be able to calculate with the mathematical phrase "5 + 7" is to be able to find the intersection of a particular row of this table (the one indexed by "5") and a particular column (indexed by "7") and note the number written there ("12"). It is this table, then, that gives its meaning to the symbol "+." The symbol "=" acquires its meaning from the practice of writing down a sentence in which it separates the original phrase from the number found in the table. What I have now said is a cursory explanation of the *semantics* of the symbols "+" and "=": in the case of the first this is a procedure to be followed, and of the second a convention for noting the outcome of doing so. A similar simple table provides the semantics for the "·" of multiplication but procedures of a different kind lie behind the use of algebraic letters, indices, and those æsthetically delightful inventions of Leibniz',

"Σ", "$\int$" and "dy/dx". Mathematical symbols are distinctive, then, in being semantically adapted to a process of transformation that will preserve the consistency of the natural language texts in which their translations are destined to be incorporated. They are logically of a piece with what we say and write because they too have a semantics that is rooted in the material world of our experience.

Algebra

75. The motivation for further developing its mathematical extension is the great difficulty encountered in formulating interesting mathematical problems in natural language; this is well–illustrated by the following rather Babylonian extract from a problem–book of Al Quarizmi—the eponymous inventor of the algorism (or algorithm[1]):

> **Problem**: *Which square when 10 times its own side is added to it is equal to 39?*
>
> **Solution**: *Halve the added side, to get 5, and multiply it by itself, to get 25. Add this to 39 to get 64. Extract the root of this number to get 8, and subtract from it half the added side to get 3. This is the side of the square you want, which is equal to 9.*

Al Quarizmi has no doubt solved his problem by thinking in the Greek geometrical style, somewhat on the following lines. The fundamental notion involved is that of "the unknown quantity." He begins with these representations:

the square on the unknown   *10 times the unknown*

---

[1] The curious lisping "th" seems to have been introduced into the word to assimilate it to "arithmetic." *Vide* OED *s.v.* "algorism."

We are given that they have a combined area of 39. But the rectangle can be dissected in this manner.

the square on the unknown   twice five times the unknown

The three pieces can be reassembled as the much beloved *gnomon* of the Greeks, still, of course, with area 39. When a square—which will, of course, have to be of side 5 to fit—is added to complement the gnomon the unknown length is seen to be 3, *i.e.* the difference between 8 and 5.

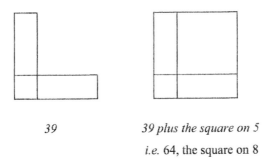

39   *39 plus the square on 5*
                      i.e. 64, the square on 8

The first step in the direction of algebra was the introduction of a shorthand which, in examples abbreviating the language of Italy, which led the field in these developments, *co* (abbreviating *cosa*) was used for the unknown *thing*, and *ce* for the *square* of *co*. With only a little further abbreviation—but crucially introducing a single letter for what had been *co*—we arrive at our modern version:

Problem: $x^2 + 10x = 39$
Solution: $x = \sqrt{(5^2 + 39)} - 5$

Here the problem is posed as a mathematical sentence of the form "(right hand side) = (left hand side)" and x is the unknown in that what is required is to

178

transform this sentence into one of the form "$x = \ldots$." The mathematical sentence has, then, this characteristic syntax: its right hand side is the grammatical subject interpreted as a quantity that is sought; its verb is the symbol "$=$"; and its grammatical predicate a complex expression that is to be transformed into a simpler quantity to be identified with the subject. What is essentially still only a piece of stenography becomes Algebra when letters are used not just for the unknown but also for the given quantities, because then problems become tokens of types whose general solutions can be sought.

Problem: $x^2 + 2ax = b$
Solution: $x = \sqrt{(a^2 + b)} - a$

Unnatural Numbers

76. Posing problems is one thing and finding their solutions is quite another. Problems can indeed easily be posed for which there is no answer—at least no answer to be found amongst the *natural numbers* whose names we use for counting. However, in such cases there may be solutions amongst unnatural numbers that we invent precisely to this end. Whereas the familiar pebbles on a beach cannot provide the semantics for such numbers, the markings on a stick, not a *tally-stick* but a *yardstick*—a piece of wood, that is, evenly divided along its length—easily can. This is a very un-Greek piece of apparatus which one cannot readily imagine Euclid picking up. However, his treatment of Number does rely upon measuring lines with segments of other lines which might in practice have been unmarked lengths of wood. As we have seen there are diagrams in his Elements in which a short segment is shown as "measuring" a longer line an integral number of times with a certain remainder, but it is with a vulgar yardstick with marked divisions that a new conception of number begins. The numeral "0," which hardly has any use in the Counting–Game can mark the beginning and then the natural numbers in turn successive divisions, as it the drawing below.

Here I have used the conventional dots to indicate that the yardstick is of indeterminate length, but below I allow it to come to an end when all the natural numbers have been exhausted; this end must be marked, just as was the beginning, and the very unnatural numeral "∞"(to be pronounced "infinity") is employed for this purpose. Here, then, is the rather unsatisfactory semantics of this new symbol.

Unsatisfactory it is because the thing depicted in the diagram clearly could not exist in the material world. Numerals which certainly have no use in counting are the names of negative numbers but they too have their semantics in a simple elaboration of the same drawing.

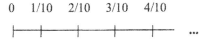

Fractions are no less unnatural than negative numbers, but in their case we can use a material yardstick as a model. Here for example is the semantics of multiples of a third.

```
0    1/3   2/3   1
├─────┼─────┼─────┤
```

This simple extension leads without difficulty by way of the division into tenths to a very significant development.

```
0    1/10   2/10   3/10   4/10
├─────┼──────┼──────┼──────┤     ...
```

180

For when the alternative decimal–point notation is substituted for these denary fractions (as in the drawing below) what emerges is *the real line*: the continuous series of the **real numbers**. Given the conventional means of presenting a magnified view of something shown elsewhere, we now have the semantics for a number which comes between any two numbers already given. Whereas the Greeks limited themselves to the discrete quantities of pebble and line segments, we now have a continuum in which numbers—the indices of the divisions of a line—lie as densely as we please.

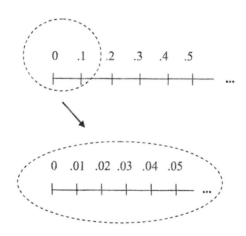

Series

77. In our treatment of Al Quarizmi's equation letters were assigned arbitrarily although a convention that has usually been observed was followed by which those standing for unknowns are chosen from the end of the Latin alphabet, whilst those for numbers given with the problem come from the beginning. When mathematicians began to interest themselves for series of numbers, more systematic assignments were made. It is not implausible to suppose this interest to have begun with the division of geometrical figures. Thus in this diagram successive coloured rectangles have the areas of a half, a quarter, an eighth, and a

sixteenth, respectively, of the containing square, the unit square, and we could go on forever dividing the not yet coloured area by the same procedure.

The area that has been coloured is 1/2 + 1/4 + 1/8 + 1/16 of the whole, and the equation the mathematician would write—using the symbolic resources currently available to him (which we will suppose already include our system for writing down the natural-language names of fractions)—in seeing that the entire square would have been coloured were he able to complete the process is the following:

$$1/2 + 1/4 + 1/8 + 1/16 + \ldots = 1.$$

This is an abbreviation for what could not be written out in full, as the dots are intended to indicate. More precisely, what they indicate here is that the process of summation is to be thought of as actually having been completed. This is, however, a very imprecise idea to which we shall have occasion to return. Mathematicians explain what is intended by saying that 1 is the **limit** of this sum which is meaningful when the diagram above is considered again: we can *see* that had the process been taken to its conclusion, the entire square would have been covered. The totality of this covering is, then, the *limit* of the process. It is this insight that saves the notion from meaninglessness.

No advance is made in the efficacy of symbolization by assigning arbitrary letters to members of the series in this fashion,

$$a + b + c + d + \ldots = 1$$

but things are very different when a systematic assignment such as the following is devised in which numbers are used as suffixes to keep each term in the series in its place:

$$a_1 + a_2 + a_3 + a_4 + \ldots = 1.$$

The use of a letter instead of a number enables an arbitrary member to be considered,

$$a_1 + a_2 + \ldots + a_i + \ldots = 1$$

and when further abbreviation is sought a powerful new symbolic device has emerged:

$$\Sigma_i \, a_i = 1.$$

The whole meaning of "$\Sigma_i \, a_i$" is contained in this sequence of abbreviated equations. Its meaning having been grasped the particular series which is in question can be specified by replacing the general term with its own proper symbol. First, however, another very powerful abbreviation is needed. The process of dividing the square above consists in always halving the area that is left. Having seen this we can rewrite

$$1/2 + 1/4 + 1/8 + 1/16 + \ldots = 1.$$

as

$$\tfrac{1}{2} + (\tfrac{1}{2} \cdot \tfrac{1}{2}) + (\tfrac{1}{2} \cdot \tfrac{1}{2} \cdot \tfrac{1}{2}) + (\tfrac{1}{2} \cdot \tfrac{1}{2} \cdot \tfrac{1}{2} \cdot \tfrac{1}{2}) + \ldots = 1.$$

The new abbreviation consists in writing $(\tfrac{1}{2})^2$ for $(\tfrac{1}{2} \cdot \tfrac{1}{2})$, $(\tfrac{1}{2})^3$ for $(\tfrac{1}{2} \cdot \tfrac{1}{2} \cdot \tfrac{1}{2})$, and so on. In general, the mathematician exploits this process of *exponentiation* by writing "a^i" for the result of multiplying a by itself i times over. In the examples above the exponent, i, is the number of times "½" appears within parentheses. This semantic observation gives the value ½ to the complex symbol $(½)^1$. The fully abbreviated expression demonstrates very well the marvellous economy and precision that is achieved with an appropriate symbolism, *viz*:

$$\Sigma_i \, (½)^{\,i} = 1.$$

Here it is to be understood that the sum in question is the limit that would be attained were, *per impossibile*, the procedure to be completed. This is made explicit by employing ∞ as the index of the last member of the series that would then have been counted. This complex of symbols can then specify the process envisaged by the calculator:

$$\Sigma_i \, (½)^{\,i} = 1$$
Lim i - ∞

What has just been presented is the game of successive abbreviation that gives this complex its meaning; *the semantics of* Σ (as well as that of an exponent) has now been explained—and an illustration given of the general process of mathematical symbolization. The important point to be noted (and to be sought in the cases of other symbols) is the generative semantic rôle of a geometrical diagram.

Infinitesimals

78. The first diagrams to be considered when the semantics of the most powerful of all symbolic innovations, the calculus, is in question are the *graphs* of Nicholas Oresme. The purpose of this XIV Century bishop in his diagrams was scientific rather than mathematical in that he wanted to make it possible to grasp the *properties* of things in an intuitive way by their *pictorial representation*. These properties would already be implicit in some collection of **data** (say of the speed

of some moving object at different times) and might well be exhibited in a table in which the speeds and times *co-ordinated* with one another were shown in different columns in the same row.

extension	intension
...	...
...	...
...	...

The columns contained the *intensions* of a quality (the speed of the motion of a projectile, for example) and the *extension* at which it was *measured* (the point in time or space). Nicholas hardly had the measuring instruments necessary to produce a very convincing table so that his investigation must have been conceptual rather than empirical; for him, no less than for us, however, it was clear that pictures are the only locus of human understanding worthy of the name.

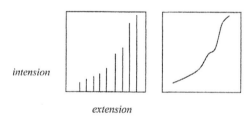

Accordingly he drew what he called *latitudes* to represent the *extensions* taken out of such a table and *longitudes* to representing the co-ordinated *intensions*. In doing so he exploited the line as the representation of the continuum of numbers. The picture is improved by smoothly connecting the measured longitudes at each latitude and when the lower and lefthand margins themselves become the real line of numbers we have the lines—now called its *axes*—of what is recognizably a modern graph. What a graph does is to show the dependency of one *quantity* (the intension for whose value we conventionally use the variable y) upon another (the extension denoted by x) and when bare numerical values are abstracted from these quantities what has become visible is a mathematical *function*.

The function certainly exists as the entity whose graph has now been drawn— as the reification of what is pictured by the graph. Before becoming visible in this manner the function might already have existed for the mathematician not merely as a table of co–ordinated numbers but as an algebraic equation; when this is the case the function can be said to be *analytic*. There is perhaps a sense in which the analytic function $x^2 + 10x$ existed for Al Quarizmi, but if so it was only as a problem for calculation. However, in being made *visible* it becomes an entity in its own right and so available for the modelling activity of scientific thinkers. But for it to becomes a tractable mathematical object it is not enough to give it a name (such as f); what the mathematician soon feels the need for is the means of specifying the value that the function has at each point on its graph: in his parlance the x co–ordinate of a point on the graph must be explicitly co–ordinated with its y co–ordinate. This is done by introducing the characteristic notational device of the algebraic extension of natural language and designating that co–ordinate by f(x), so that Al Quarizmi's problem becomes the determination of what the unknown quantity x must be for f(x) to be 39. In the parlance of mathematicians what the graph shows is that 39 is the *value* of the function for the *argument* 3.

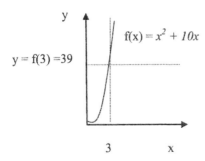

The fundamental game that can be played with a **graph**—the ultimate semantic basis, that is, of the game of symbols we call "the Calculus"—is one invented (like so much else in our story) in Ancient Greece. Eudoxus was the player whose name is particularly associated with this so–called *method of exhaustion*. As a famous application of it he calculated the area of a circle by considering those of a polygon within which the circle is inscribed and of one inscribed within the circle. In my diagram we see the circle nestled loosely between two squares and also somewhat more tightly between two octagons. Two 16–sided polygons would squeeze it rather more closely, 32–sided ones even more so, and so on.

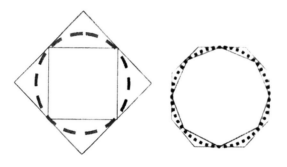

The picture makes it clear that the area lies somewhere between those of the circumscribed and inscribed polygons—and, equally clearly, that as the number of sides of the polygons is increased the area of each more nearly approaches that of the circle. Indeed, by sufficiently increasing the number of their sides the difference between the areas of the polygons and of the circle contained within them can be made arbitrarily small, thereby constraining it within as small an interval as may be desired. And here is the application of the notion of a *limit* crucial to the development of the calculus: a judgement can be made about what the area of the circle really is by supposing the polygons to have so many sides that they have themselves become indistinguishable from circles. "π" is the name we now give to the dimensionless ratio of the square on a radius of the circle to this *limiting* value, and in giving it a name it is brought into being as a new mathematical object. To apply this same method to the area between the graph and its horizontal axis, the calculator divides it into vertical strips and considers the rectangles whose upper ends contain the graph (i) from above, and (ii) from below.

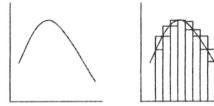

The Σ-symbol having been introduced into his repertoire and the notion of a limit also being available the area sought can be expressed as the limiting sum of a series. This sum is given a symbol, I, and so reified in its turn as the *integral* of the function. But the series in question are very difficult to sum and the real power of the symbolic advances that constitute the calculus is not unleashed until a different approach to the study of graphs is adopted. This emerges when the mathematician concerns himself with the *tangents* to the graph—with straight lines, that is, which touch it at a particular point without cutting through it. The interesting property of a tangent is its *slope, i.e.* the distance points on the line ascend vertically within the picture plane as they move horizontally across it. When the symbol Δx is introduced to denote the horizontal distance between two given points on the line, so that if one has x as its horizontal co-ordinate that of the other—exploiting the symbolic resources now available—can be written as *(x+Δx)*, the vertical distance between them can be written as *f(x+ Δx) – f(x)*.

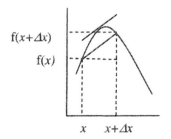

The significant advance that follows is to introduce a new symbol, df/dx, whose form is that of a fractional number (as might be used in specifying the three–tenths gradient of a road that climbed three feet for every ten it advanced). It is **defined** to be an abbreviation for the following:

$$Lim \ (f(x + \Delta x) - f(x) \ )/\Delta x$$
$$\Delta x - 0$$

in which the limit is readily understood to be that in which Δx becomes infinitesimally small. The meaning given to the symbol, df/dx, is reified as the *differential* of the function f. What is important for our present purpose is its semantics: it is only in virtue of the drawing above that it has its initial meaning.

This meaning is, however, elaborated when "df/dx" is put to mathematical work, and its first important rôle is to modify the notion of the integral of the same function. The way in which this is done further illuminates the semantics of mathematics. The integral of the function f must first be recognized as itself a *function*. As such it too can be named by a letter; "F" will serve our present purpose. A useful function is defined in this manner,

$$F(x) = \int^x f,$$

which is intended to make the value of the new function at some co–ordinate the area under the graph from the origin up to just that point. With this new function in mind, the mathematician now considers again the graph of the original function.

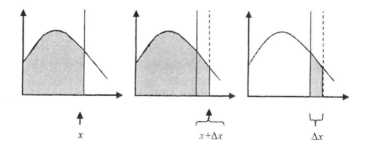

What he does in considering it is something that could not even be conceived without the symbolic advances that have just been explained. He considers a point a short distance beyond x on the axis; the short distance he calls "Δx," so that this symbol designates some indefinite real number and he *sees* that the difference between the value of $F(x)$, the shaded area in the first drawing of f, and $F(x+\Delta x)$, the shaded area in the second drawing, is just the area shaded in the third. This area has a value that lies somewhere between $f(x)\Delta x$ and $f(x+\Delta x)\Delta x$ and so is not significantly different from $f(x)\Delta x$ in the limit where Δx is very small. All this is, as I stressed, to be *seen* in the diagrams. But what follows is a matter of purely symbolic manipulation. The mathematician writes down the equation that has just been explained,

$$F(x+\Delta x) - F(\Delta x) = f(x)\Delta x,$$

and then rearranges it by the rules of ordinary algebra as

$$(F(x+\Delta x) - F(\Delta x)) / \Delta x = f(x).$$

He then recognizes, as we do, the expression on the left hand side as the quantity by which, supposing it to be evaluated in the limit in which Δx is vanishingly small, dF/dx would be defined. But F is nothing other than the integral of f, so that what the mathematician has grasped in this syntactico–semantic manner is the so–called *Fundamental theorem of the Calculus*, *viz.* that integration and differentiation are inverse operations and, in particular, that integration is nothing other than anti–differentiation. This is not something that can be *seen* in any picture; it is only discovered by playing with symbols that themselves derive their initial meanings—as we have insisted all symbols do—from pictures.

Play with pictures leads in its turn to the introduction of further symbols whose use cannot always be foreseen. Thus having acquired the notion of the gradient of a function one can imagine (and indeed attempt to draw) a function whose gradient is everywhere the same as its value. This condition is easily written down in symbolic terms as $f(x) = df(x)/dx$. Amongst the functions very amenable to mathematical analysis are those which can now be expressed using

190

the device of exponentiation, the simplest of which are x^2, x^3, ..., and so on, or, in general, x^n. The differentials of these functions are the easiest of all to calculate and the general result is found to be that $d(x^n)/dx = n \cdot x^{(n-1)}$. But this having been seen, the exponential function can also be written down, for when the series

$$1 + x + x^2/2 + x^3/(2 \cdot 3) + x^4/(2 \cdot 3 \cdot 4) + ...$$

is differentiated term by term using this general rule, the result is exactly the same series. The exponential function is abbreviated in its term using the symbol e^x which occurs very frequently in the writings of scientists. When x is the number 1, the sum of the series is a little over 2.7 which is, then, the value of e^1 *i.e.* of a number e to put alongside π as another not so mysterious mathematical symbol.

Numerical Geometry

79. The linear representation of number is put to powerful use by Descartes. He superimposes the axes of a graph upon the picture surface on which Euclid makes his drawings of geometrical figures.

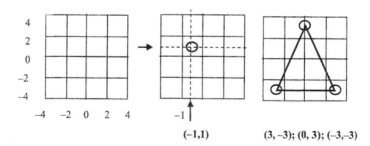

(−1,1)   (3, −3); (0, 3); (−3,−3)

By this means the surface becomes a two dimensional analogue of the yardstick whose divisions we identified earlier as the semantic basis of the system of real numbers. A grid is now in place on the picture plane which allows a unique couple of numbers—(−1,1), for example—to be assigned to each of its points. When the figures which are the essential accompaniments of a Euclidean proof have been drawn on the surface and the vertices of each identified in this way with a couple of numbers, the lines or curves connecting them are segments of the graphs of functions. To completely simulate geometrical drawing in this arithmetical manner, some number must be assigned to the distance between two points and this is done using the Pythagorean relationship between the sides and hypotenuse of the right–triangle from which the co–ordinates are read off. Thus if the difference in the x co–ordinates of two points is, say, 4 and that of their y co–ordinates 3, then the distance between them can be calculated to be 5 units (as in the diagram).

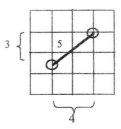

In algebraic geometry the Pythagorean theorem of Euclid's presentation has become a *tautology*. It is in this way—and not by arranging pebbles in geometrical patterns—that the mathematics of discrete and continuous quantities is seen to be one and the same thing. For if the *distance* between any two of the points which are now ordered pairs of *numbers* is defined by this Pythagorean relationship, then otherwise intractable geometrical problems are easily solved because the algebraic expressions for lines, and circles, and so on, enable points of intersection to be *calculated*. The mathematician can henceforth do his geometry by *calculation* and he can often do so quite mechanically without relying upon any insight into the meanings of the symbols he is manipulating. At least in its routine application mathematics becomes divorced from intuition.

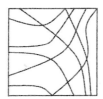

But this is only a beginning to the conceptual and computational power that Descartes has unlocked, for having produced in the manner of the drawing above a representation of a geometrical plane, the mathematician can distort it (in the manner of the drawing above) to represent a surface that is not flat but curved. He cannot, however, apply the same symbolic apparatus to the geometry of such a surface until he has some three–dimensional analogue of the Cartesian plane.

Perspective

80. With the Renaissance the systematic thinking that is characteristic of Science was also applied to painting (whose greatest practitioners were, indeed, not infrequently also mathematical innovators). What is novel and very distinctive in this art is the precise use of perspective to create the illusion of depth on a plane canvas. The fundamental observation is that things appear not only less intensely coloured but also smaller to us the further away from us they are. This can be exploited by a painter who is not at all mathematically minded by simply organizing the things he paints as foreground elements (like the bison in the picture below), or elements of the middle–ground (the pale tree), or back–ground (the very pale distant mountains) and progressively reducing their sizes on the canvas.

More mathematically minded picture–makers were able to discern the rules for producing an illusion of continuous recession in Space by studying the appearance of colonnades, or the flagstones paving a courtyard, or the tiled interiors of palaces. And this illusion projected onto the two–dimensional picture surface which is (as we have insisted) the real locus of human understanding is what is needed to provide the semantics first for an analogue of our two–dimensional graphs and secondly for geometrical Space itself. The diagram drawn below which shows—with something like the foreshortening of perspective—three orthogonally disposed planes, each ruled with a co–ordinate grid suggests how a point in Euclidean space can become a triplet of numbers—e.g. (5, 6, –5).

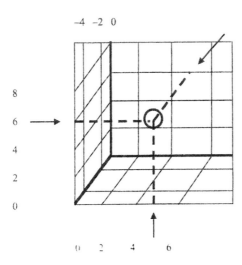

The mechanical rules for doing geometry on the Euclidean plane can be applied in the three dimensional space illustrated here. The same rules then become the vehicle for escaping the bounds of the space of our experience, for they are then very easily extended to geometrical constructions of what the mathematicians calls **manifolds** of four– or five– or, indeed as many dimensions as we please—even an infinity of them. Whilst none of these manifolds can be shown in a picture of any kind, they can be explored in a purely symbolic manner and their features and properties discovered. The only *understanding* that this mechanical extrapolation of an original two–dimensional semantics can bring is when some three–dimensional section of the higher–dimensional manifold containing whatever has been discovered is projected onto a two–dimensional picture surface.

Complex Space

81. The momentous event that has now occurred is that the Space that was the matrix for the construction of triangles and squares has acquired a purely mathematical existence as a continuum of sets of numbers—the (1,2) and so on of algebraic plane geometry, or the (1,2,3) *etc.* of algebraic spatial geometry. It only remains to see this continuum as nothing more than precisely the stuff upon which symbolic operations are carried out for the way to be open to inventing new ways of manipulating it that are derived neither from our experience of counting nor from that of making geometrical constructions. These new operations consist in manipulating the symbols under the constraints of the semantics we have discussed above, but the symbols themselves can seem to have been set free by the mechanical rules for their employment. I want to say, however, that if they are not to be *meaningless* (in a precise sense to which I shall shortly return) the invented objects must nevertheless be suggested by something that can be pictured. This is certainly true of the most important of them all, *viz.* those that constitute a *vector space.*

For the mathematician a vector is nothing more than a set of numbers, so that the couples and triplets of numbers that are the Cartesian co-ordinates of points are the particular vectors known as *position vectors* (one can also see single numbers as vectors with only one component), but the idea he has in mind in inventing the operations to be performed on them can only be that of an arrow attached to some fixed point. This arrow is the vector which is the same set of numbers that would be the co-ordinates of its tip were this the Euclidean space of ordinary experience. All the constituent arrows of a vector space are attached to the same point (the "origin" of the space). Each vector is given a name, a symbol such as "**a**" or "**b**". Vectors can be stretched along their own length by the operation of *scalar multiplication* that multiplies each number in the set by the same number, so that the symbols "3**a**" or "4**b**," for example, are given their meanings. And so is "−**a**," the vector a multiplied by −1: this is the same vector with its direction reversed. Vectors cannot be added as numbers are by consulting an addition table, but to make such formulæ as "**a** + **b**" meaningful, the mathematician invents an operation of composition for them which makes this sum the diagonal of the parallelogram in vector space whose respective sides are the vectors **a** and **b** (as in the next drawing). In this way an equation written with the new, unnatural numbers such as "**a** + **b** = **c**" has its meaning and there is a use for the symbol "×" to designate the unknown vector in such a vector–algebra formula. The operations of vector–addition and scalar–multiplication allow the mathematician to designate a pair of vectors to be the *basis* of the vector–space in the sense that any other vector can be composed by adding together certain scalar multiples of them. He also multiplies them by making their product the area of the same parallelogram (the shaded region in the last drawing below), but for this area to be a vector it must be understood to be directed: the vector **d** which is equal to **a** × **b** has one of the directions perpendicular to the surface (which of the two is carefully specified) and a length numerically equal to that of its area.

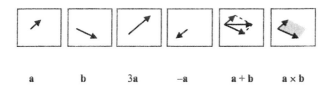

     a   **b**   3**a**   −**a**   **a** + **b**   **a** × **b**

These vectors, these ordered sets of numbers, are still far from being the end of the *abstraction* in which the mathematician delights. The space in which he ultimately lets his imagination roam free does indeed consists of numbers but the positive and negative real numbers are hardly more adequate for his adventures than the natural numbers with which he began. Many of the equations that he writes down as problems for solution involve—not as acceptable answers, but in the course of their solution—the square roots of negative numbers. The situation in which the mathematician finds himself is this: if he is to solve these equations at all, then he must pretend to himself underway that negative numbers do have square roots. In order to be able to manipulate such things he invents the

196

mathematical objects called *complex–numbers*. Each of these is—somewhat like a vector—a couple of real numbers. Together they are the denizens to a space called the Complex Plane which is spanned by one entity said to be *real* and another said to be *imaginary*. The first is the real number 1 whilst its imaginary companion is the square–root of the real negative number −1 (whose numeral is the famous symbol *i*). These complex numbers are the veritable stuff of algebra; their invention allows all the equations that can be written down using letters to represent real numbers to be solved. The mathematician not only calls them "numbers" but treats them entirely as such: he invents functions whose arguments and values are complex numbers and even vectors whose components are similarly complex. He finds ways of differentiating and integrating all these unnatural things. The mathematician is himself strongly disinclined to acknowledge that diagrams such as ours have anything to do with his complex vector algebra or, indeed, that any of the diagrams in this chapter have, in general, very much to do with his use of symbols: they are all, he will tell you, merely props for the man with insufficient genuine mathematical intuition.

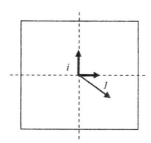

As we shall see, however, it is precisely this semantic foundation that makes his algebra *meaningful* to the scientist in that it is the very condition for his ability to exploit it as an essential component of his own scientific thinking. And it is moreover very difficult to see what meaning a complicated formula can have without his being mindful of the same semantic basis. There is, for example, a famous expression, often known as *Euler's Formula,* which relates several mathematical symbols in what seems at first sight a mysterious way. The symbols in question (whose semantics we have considered above) are the unnatural number "−1," its square-root "i," "π," which stands, as we saw, for the ratio of the circumference of a circle to its diameter, and "e," the exponential number appearing in the function e^x introduced above whose derivative for any argument is equal to its value. Euler's Formula is "$e^{i\pi} = -1$;" what it would seem to say is, then, that *when one is taken away from nothing, the result is the same as when the exponential number is raised to the power of the product of the square-root of one less than nothing and the ratio of the circumference of any circle to its own diameter.* This must come as close as any English sentence to utterly impenetrable meaninglessness. This impression is, however, dispelled as soon as the lesson of this chapter is taken to heart and it is recognized that the symbols are to be interpreted upon the basis of their own semantics and not upon that of ordinary English words. I do not think it could be meaningful at all without this recognition. As we saw above, when x stands for a real number, the symbol e^x stands for the sum of a series in which each term is derived from its predecessor by multiplying it by x and dividing it by the next natural number.

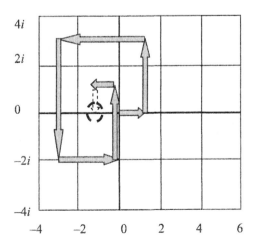

We see, then, that in the case of a *real number* (greater than 1) the semantic basis of the meaningfulness of "e^x" is a movement along a measuring rod in steps that decrease in size very rapidly so that the process quickly comes to a halt. If x had the value of π, for example, then the points reached on the yardstick starting from its beginning would be first 1 and then (very roughly) those marked with 4, 9, 14, 18, 21, 22, 23 and so on. But in the case of the *complex number* which is the exponent in Euler's formula, *i.e.* not π, but $i\pi$, the rectangular spiral path shown in the diagram above is traced out through the complex plane. This path quickly converges upon the point which represents the real number −1 and therein lies Euler's entire—and no longer quite so mysterious—meaning.

Summary

82. In this chapter I have tried to explain the semantic basis of the symbolic language of the mathematician. Whereas the most familiar symbols (those adopted earliest in the history of mathematics) were shown to be mere abbreviations for numerals and other words in the Latin sentences that thereby became mathematical formulæ, all others derive their meanings from games that are played with number symbols (the addition– and multiplication–games being the originals). It was shown how the yardstick can be regarded as the semantic basis for the numbers used in counting which become the *natural numbers* when such *unnatural numbers* as 0, −1, and ∞ are adopted together with fractions, decimals and rational numbers, all with the same yardstick as their foundation. Because of their importance for understanding both the emergence of modern Science and the relationship of the whole of Science to Mathematics, close attention was played to the geometrical diagrams which supply the original semantics for the *infinitesimal calculus*. The *Cartesian transformation* of Geometry into Algebra was also explained as was that of pictures in *perspective* because of their importance for understanding the notion of *mathematical modelling* which will soon be shown to have an essential rôle to play in the scientific method. We are now in a position properly to appreciate in the sequel

how the power of symbolization is allied with the deliverances of insight discussed in the previous chapter.

THEORY

The Euclidean Paradigm

83. There is a sense of the word in which a *model* is something prescriptive. It is in this sense that a woman on a catwalk can be a model by showing her scatter-brained sisters how the fashion industry would like them to dress. Euclid's writings are an exercise in mathematics and not science, but through two millennia his scheme of explanation has been the model for the scientific ampliation of knowledge: ever since his time it has been the road to understanding that rational thinkers ought to follow. In each of his proofs the construction intended by Euclid is not a particular drawing but a type of drawing (its size and proportions not being specified). Examining, with Euclid as guide, the drawing that accompanies his text we attain a certain insight: we become aware of something that is invariant across all tokens of the type. But this insight is useless (it cannot be extracted from the drawing and applied elsewhere) until it has been given linguistic expression. This comes in the form of a geometrical *law*. In the case of the Windmill-drawing discussed in an earlier chapter this is the law that we learned to recite as small children and which is what we primarily associate with Pythagoras, *viz. that the square on the hypotenuse is equal to the sum of the squares on the other two sides*. This particular case illustrates well what is essential to a geometrical law, *i.e.* its economy in classifying and summarizing a

202

multitude of interesting facts with application in the world of our ordinary experience—not just that the 3-4-5 triangle has the Pythagorean property, then, but that so too do the 5-12-13, 7-24-25, and countless others which the pyramid-builders might also have used.

Euclid's concern was not for the material triangle but for something that it only represents: something that not only transcends matter but, to the cast of mind we call *Platonic*, is more *real* than anything material.

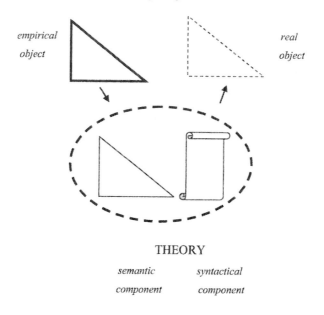

empirical object

real object

THEORY

semantic component

syntactical component

The diagram above puts all the features of the venerable Euclidean model in their places; they are

> (1) an **empirical object**: *in the case we have been considering of the Pythagorean Theorem, a material object whose shape is a right-angled triangle—e.g. the stretched rope of an Egyptian surveyor;*

> (2) *a representation of this, consisting of two components: a construction (a drawing in ink on paper), the **semantic** object that*

*makes the theory meaningful and from which insight derives, and a text, the **syntactical** object in which the same insight is articulated and warranted;* together with

(3) *a **real object**: the type of which all empirical triangles are mere tokens.*

Having recognized that a geometrical law is a pronouncement applied primarily not to Euclid's drawings nor to anybody else's, and certainly not to ropes strung out across the desert by Pharaoh's builders, we moderns are more inclined to say that *where the law rules is in our understanding,* so that we can make use of it as a guide in such mundane doings of our own as building pyramids. From the drawing we derive *inarticulate insight;* the theoretical proof articulates this insight and shows it not to be illusory. Without the model the theorem has no meaning; without the proof the insight derived from it has no validity. Insight and validity are the two sides of a single coin, its *semantic* and *syntactical* sides. This syntactico-semantic coin is scientific *understanding.*

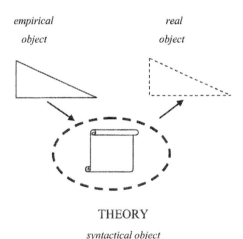

empirical
object

real
object

THEORY

syntactical object

As philosophers investigating the notion of "science" we can, however, very easily be misled, because *the material construction—the drawing on a page of Euclid's book—is itself an instance (or* representative*) of the empirical reality* it represents. It can seem, then, that there is nothing more to Euclid's model than its syntactical component, the written theorem. This leads to a misapprehension of the Euclidean model (to not really grasping what the girl on the catwalk has on, as it were). It is perhaps only in the case of the scientific study of the mathematical objects that we call *numbers* and *geometrical figures* that such confusion is possible, but many philosophers and scientists have supposed that the degenerate scheme suggested in this second diagram was Euclid's own and so—given the impressive certainty of the results he obtained—the paradigm by which scientists should be guided. This error is the basis of the misguided *Syntactical Concept of Science* which it will be my next task to describe more fully.

To that end it will be worthwhile now to review the paradigmatic path to understanding that I reconstructed (albeit somewhat conjecturally) in earlier chapters. The starting point was what?—not the drawing with which I began; we can go further back than that to what we call an **idea**. This seems to be something like a drawing but one done in the imagination (what Kant called a **pure intuition**). Drawing done in the imagination can easily seem to have the same sort of necessity that Plato could only locate in his heaven but for those of us moderns who think like Kant it seems rather to derive from this being how human imagination happens to do things. How does one draw in the imagination?— Despite the best efforts of psychologists and philosophers there is hardly anything more to be said than to note that *imaginary* drawing very easily overflows to become *real* drawing: when we are imagining a triangle we can easily find ourselves (without making much of a conscious decision so to do) also moving our hands in the air or even, if pen and paper at for hand, really drawing one[1]. (I am not sure that I can do it at all without making at least minute movements of my

---

[1] For the details of this process as I understand it, see again the first pages of my *Genesis of Meaning*.

eyes.) It is recorded that around the year 400 of our epoch Augustine was amazing his contemporaries by his ability to read without saying his words out loud; in the XVI Century Bacon similarly amazed his by reading without even moving his lips. *Doing and thinking seem to be very much the same.* Thinking is always *doing* that is at least continent. It is because we sometimes find that what we supposed ourselves to have drawn in imagination cannot quite be drawn on paper that we learn to trust only what we have done in the material world. Here is our reconstruction.

(1) *Hypothesis: Euclid's real starting point was a relationship amongst the lengths of the sides of a right-triangle that practical men were able to apply to their work with assured success. There was something that seemed to him to be the case.*

(2) *Imagination: With the intention of satisfying himself that it really was the case, he must have considered, in the space of imagination, an arrangement of triangles and squares amongst which this relationship obtained.*

(3) *Construction: Having made the immaterial construction his next step was to allow his continent thought to overflow in making a material construction to represent what until then had existed only in imagination, to move it from imaginary space into the space of human doing. In my conjectural reconstruction he did this by tearing out some triangles and squares from a sheet of paper and manipulating them on his table top. He did all this, and, as it seems to me, it was in this* doing *that his understanding emerged.*

(4) **Proof:** *On the basis of this construction and in a play of the logic game discussed above he then composed his famous proof to convince himself and us that he really had done what he thought he had. The drawing that he must have had in front of him as he composed (together, of course, with the semantics of his native Greek) gave the proof the meaning it has. This proof is highly artificial with a drawing contrived especially to serve its purposes.*

(5) **Enunciation:** *Recognizing his own doing as the token of a type of drawings based upon right triangles of any shape Euclid enunciated the general proposition he had proved in this way as a* law *intelligible in ordinary language,* i.e. *he affirmed the rectitude of his original hypothesis.*

The jurisdiction of this law is the *material realm*, so that it can be applied by those who know nothing of the theory and—given the authority of Mathematics and the corroboration of repeated successful applications—used by them with confidence in, for example, pyramid-building. Taken out of its context, then, the law is something of a black-box: one puts in, let us say, the number 3 and 4, and one gets another number out, in that case 5. One sees nothing whatsoever of what is going on inside the box; that a 3-4-5 triangle can be used by a builder is more than enough for those who are not called to be systematic thinkers. For the builder the law is tested in its being applied, i.e. the black-box either works or it does not. But for the scientific thinker the proof must give a guarantee. If a builder made use of a 3-4-5 triangle in setting out his pyramid and the finished edifice was deformed, and not orthogonally symmetrical, then the fault could only be the builder's own and not Euclid's—*unless, of course, there happens to be something wrong with our proof-constructing logic or even with our world-categorizing language—or (and it was hardly before the time of the mathematician Gauss that this possibility was seriously entertained)—with Euclid's axioms.* Given the same proviso the law applies equally to drawings we make in the space of the imagination (it is because constructions in the two spaces are so alike that it seems unnecessary to even

207

mention this). If we do imagine drawings to which it does not apply, then we can be sure we have only *seemed* to imagine them.

Modernization

84. We must look carefully at what it is the *scientist* does in attempting to follow this Euclidean paradigm—and that is best done in recalling the origins of that procedure. Before scientific method emerged thinking in Europe was in terms of Aristotelian *qualities*. Each unexplained phenomenon encountered was explained by indicating a novel quality inherent in the things implicated, so that in saying that an essential quality of lodestone is the magnetic quality an understanding would already have been achieved. One might then have said that the quality of orthogonality was part of the essence of the 3-4-5 triangle of the Egyptians. The *analytic* conception of science that supplanted this useless Aristotelianism deals with qualities (heat, magnetism, weight, and so on) as measurable intensities— and so as *quantities*; it is instructive to review how it was attained.

Science begins, of course, with a curious taking note of the world about us, but the mere collection of voluminous data is not in itself a recognizable manifestation of scientific activity. What is characteristic of this activity is the particular way in which data is presented: it must be turned into the occasion of the formation of hypotheses by which is meant, just as in our epitome of Euclid's procedure, a candidate for confirmation as a law not this time of transcendental reality but of empirical Nature. It seemed to Francis Bacon that the appropriate way of treating observational data is to arrange them in *tables* of variations in the co-presence of the different properties of things. The virtue of a table is that we can *look at* it in the hope to *seeing* something not otherwise apparent. Tables are visual models of collections of data and allow generalizations to be carefully made or rejected; the importance of their giving the scientist something to look at is not to be underestimated, for the practice of turning tables into the even more perspicuous models of data we know as *graphs* is an indispensible step on the road to Science. Before a graph can be drawn, however, the properties to be investigated had to be transformed from qualities into measurable quantities. In making such a model axes are associated with properties suspected of dependence upon one another and items of data are plotted in the area they span. To this end points on the axes must correspond with definite numerical values that measurements can take. In the space of the graph, then, a visual model of a collection of data is constructed. The tables that were of the greatest significance for the emergence of Science were the observations published by Ptolemy of the apparent positions of the planets as they moved onward, and occasionally back, across the sphere of the fixed stars. The matrix of his thought being the Greek *Weltanschauung* discussed above Ptolemy could not conceive of eternal motion that was anything other than circular and he was led to the complex system of cycles and epicycles with which we associate his name.

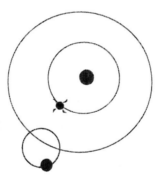

Given that the planets were understood to be embedded in crystalline shells encircling the earth it seems hardly credible that he can have supposed this system to be physically real, but however that may be, we clearly recognize his system as a *mathematical model* that serves no other end than to *save the phenomena*. But modern Science emerges as Kepler pores over these endless tables—or rather the very precise versions compiled by Tycho Brahe—in what seems to us a mighty effort to *see* what physical reality they might conceal. He may well have been motivated by that aversion to complexity that is the real hallmark of the analytic intellect and to which the Scholastics gave expression in the familiar tag *simpliciter sigillum veritatis*[2], for his thinking is in many respects hardly modern.

It is appropriate to say that it was *as* he did this that Science emerged because at the beginning he was very clearly looking not with the eyes of a scientist but with those of a Platonic mystic. What he was prepared to see was the precise way in which the divine intelligence that had ordered the heavens had arranged the orbits of the six planets visible to the naked eye. This ordering must be *perfect* but also *intelligible* which indicated to Kepler that the spheres upon which the planets moved must somehow be placed so that *we* should be able to construct (and the whole of Euclid's effort can be seen as directed to showing us how this was to be done) Platonic solids to fit nicely between them. It was his repeated failure to find anything satisfactory of this sort in Ptolemy's data that started Kepler thinking as a scientist. He was still looking for geometrical form in the data but he no longer supposed he already knew what it must be. What he found to his astonishment was that if the planets are moving with uniform speed, then their orbits are not circles centred on the earth but ellipses focussed on the sun.

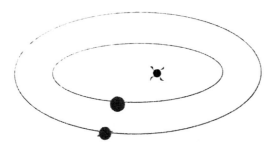

An ellipse is the appearance of a circle looked at obliquely (it is, as we observed earlier, how a circular orbit would appear to a God placed a long way off to the side in his heaven, glancing casually down at some mere corner of his creation) and Kepler could convince himself that such motion is very *simple* by comparison

---

[2] *i.e.* that simplicity is the very hallmark of truth.

with Ptolemy's proposal. What is restored, indeed, is Aristotelian uniformity in that, just as in pure circular motion without epicycles, the planet's movement along its path is such that the radius from the sun sweeps out the same area in equal intervals of time.

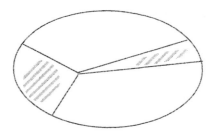

Kepler also found that the simplicity latent in the distances of the planetary orbits from the sun was just as simple but of a quite un-Platonic kind: it can only be expressed as a mathematical *function*[3], something merely to be calculated with until a way was found to make it *visible* when it became an entity in its own right.

The Newtonian Paradigm

85. The scientist is concerned not with the transcendental realm of Platonic *ideas* or Kantian *pure intuition*, but with that of *empirical intuition*: the realm to which it seems to us (perhaps a little naïvely, as some troublesome philosophers would say) that we have direct access through our senses. This is the realm the philosophically untutored call *Reality, simpliciter*, because nothing could be more real than the place where we live out our short lives in such very real joy and pain. An appropriate way to compare and contrast the scientific mode of understanding with Euclid's geometrical method—one often employed by historians of Science—is to reconstruct the first and greatest recognizably *scientific* achievement in our modern sense, *viz.* Newton's celestial mechanics. What I intend is an *idealized reconstruction* in that I am not concerned with any historical

---

[3] The function discovered by Kepler in the mess of data assembled by Brahe is $\tau^2 = s^3$ where τ is the orbital period and s the semi axis of the ellipse.

sequence of events but rather with how a thinker conscious of his method would arrive at Newton's results. Here are the steps that might be followed.

*(1) The starting point could only be an **empirical intuition** of the wandering stars—the planets—which seem to circle the heavens about our own heads. But as I have insisted nothing is anything to us until we have made its picture— without our having done this there would be no stars, and no movements amongst them: in particular, there would be no revolution of the heavens. I recalled in our first chapter how, since the time of the mysterious Sumerians (who also seem to have invented writing), we have made pictures of the heavens at different times and dates in which we label the planets with the names by which we refer to them in ordinary language. Such pictures would be considered by a scientist who reflected upon the matter to be representations of an intuition of empirical reality (as we have seen, however, there are philosophical reasons for regarding this point of view as somewhat naïve).*

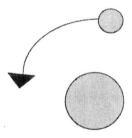

empirical intuition

(2) A model intended to have the same structure as this representation would be constructed. We have hesitated to describe Euclid's drawing of triangles and squares as a model but we do find ourselves quite naturally saying something of the sort when we have a scientific theory before us. The scientist's models can be constructed in either of two ways which can seem quite distinct: it is a mathematical model that is characteristic of Science, but

*there is always an antecedent intuitive one and the passage from the first to the second is by way of the insight to which we devoted a chapter above. One **intuitive model** of the heavens also contemplated by the astrologer (the famous one invented by Eudoxus and elaborated by Aristotle) consists of globes of fire embedded in concentric spherical shells and a Prime Mover that sets them all in motion. This structure is readily imagined and can also be drawn on paper or, of course, put into words. But this will not do for a Newton precisely because it is not suitable for the passage to which we just referred. One model of the appropriate sort that makes the behaviour of the moon revolving about the earth intelligible is that of a conker on a string (I do not of course presume to know that this is what Newton himself had in mind.) The tension in the string held by an energetic schoolboy constrains his chestnut to go round in a circle, but were he to let the string go, the conker would carry on with the motion in then had and fly off at a tangent. The first element of the insight necessary to understanding is this: that it can only be the action of something analogous to this tension that keeps the moon in her orbit.*

intuitive model

The present suggestion is, then, that this analogy between empirical intuition represented in, for example, a picture of the earth and the moon seen from somewhere in Outer Space, on the one hand, and a suitable intuitive model, on the other, is the basis of Newton's understanding of celestial motion The points of analogy are the circular motion of the conker, on the one hand, and the elliptical motion of the moon, on the other, together with the force felt in the string and the unashamedly occult force that holds the moon in her orbit. The material string is a point of disanalogy for which allowance will have to be made. There are, no doubt, other intuitive models which might have been the point of departure, for there is no sense in which any model is determined by the original empirical intuition (no more, that is, than the sitter on her throne determines the picture which the artist studying her form paints on his canvas).

*(3) The characteristic scientific way of exploiting a model is to reduce it to a symbolic object, i.e. the derived mathematical model, and the model is suitable precisely to the degree it facilitates this passage. The first step in the symbolic transformation is to make a **diagram** of the intuitive model on the lines of the specimen below from which everything inessential to the emerging explanation has been expunged.*

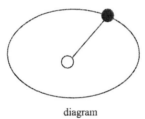

diagram

Such a diagram will serve this purpose because, as we saw in the last chapter, it is diagrams that supply the semantics for the symbol system which is the medium in which a mathematical model is constructed. Its formal similarity to those diagrams will determines the degree to which the symbolic model will simplify and distort in its turn its already simplified and distorting intuitive original or even import new unwanted elements of disanalogy that may not always be noticed. The fundamental limitation is, however, that nothing of the empirical phenomenon in question that is not represented in this diagram will be scientifically understood with its aid.

214

But now we must interrupt this specimen of scientific method because (as Newton's final result suggests) our scientist will hardly get any further by thinking exclusively of the moon in her orbit or even a little more generally of satellites in theirs. The present model gives no obvious purchase for the faculty we have called "insight" throughout this essay: what we cannot directly uncover is the hidden pattern which, once we have set our sights upon it, will make everything clear. We must examine our experience with moving things here on earth, for we have, of course, no experience to draw upon of moving the moon. What is called for, then, is a *generalization*: our Newton must consider the effect that forces generally have upon the motion of massive bodies—he must recall the apple falling from the tree and other salient examples of motion from his non-scientific experience. What our everyday experience teaches us is that we must apply a force—that of the action of our own bodies or of some powerful animal that we have harnessed—to set things in motion and, further, that the more we exert ourselves—or the harder we whip our beasts—the faster things go. It is this untutored quotidian insight that must be exploited in seeking scientific understanding of what is going on wherever it may be in the universe.

empirical intuition   *intuitive model*

As in the case of the lunar orbit suitable diagrams will hardly be drawn without making a deliberate compromise with experience, simplifying what we experience by an idealization directed towards the symbolic model whose construction is the immediate goal. Thus gross bodies must become point masses; spheres and planes become perfectly smooth and the resistance to motion of the air becomes negligible. One simple and fruitful phenomenon to model is that of a bob oscillating on a spring and the tug-of-war is a particular experience from which an *intuitive model* can be drawn to make the oscillating behaviour of the bob intelligible. The *empirical intuition* and an appropriate intuitive model for this case are represented in the pictures above. In employing these models the knot on the rope has to be identified with the bob and our insight into the familiar experience transferred to its oscillating motion. The insight in question is that the team momentarily exerting a greater force will move the knot in its own direction whilst the whole is at rest whenever the contending forces are in balance.

The general insight that could hardly be suggested by a weight on a spring alone but will be gathered from countless examples from within the whole breadth of our mundane experience—from bullocks pulling carts, from apples falling from trees, from projectiles falling to earth, from pendulums swinging on their cords, and so on—is that things are moved when the forces acting on them are out of balance and that the quantity of motion given to any one of them varies as does the unbalanced force. "Suggested" is the word I find myself using, for there is no sense in which this gathering of insight is a process of reasoning. It emerges when the attempt is made to produce diagrams of intuitive models on the lines employed here. Such diagrammatic activity is, as it seems to me, the focus of human understanding.

The scientific achievement depends upon our intuitive models of each of these experiences being recognized by us as *tokens* of a single *type*. Newton gave expression to his recognition of this by enunciating—in what is generally acknowledged by those qualified to have an opinion to be the supreme example of human genius—his so-called "Laws of Motion." The insight contained in the first law is that whenever in this world an unbalanced force is acting things are set in motion but only, as it were, reluctantly, for each has a certain heaviness. "Things," Newton proclaims, "continue in their state of rest or uniform motion unless impelled by some external force to change that state." We say in ordinary language that certain things are heavier than certain others by which we mean that the effect of applying the same force to different things is not the same. To be able to grasp the nature of this difference the notion of the "quantity of motion" is needed. We say that a heavy thing (say a runaway loaded cart) travelling at a certain speed has more motion than a lighter one (an empty cart) because experience teaches us that we must exert more of our own force to stop it. Newton formulates this trivial, universal experience in the following careful terms that make it possible to reduce this trait of ordinary experience to mathematical symbols: "the rate of change of the quantity of motion," he says, "is proportional to the force applied." This pronouncement relates force directly to motion and its semantic content is of great interest; what it does is to tell us that two things are one and the same, *viz.*, on the one hand, the application of a force to a material body, and, on the other, the change of motion in that body.

Here is the diagram that contains our understanding of the pronouncement: to the left is a material body of otherwise indeterminate character which, as the arrow is intended to indicate, is moving along; to the right is the same body to which a force (indicated by the broader arrow) is being applied, thereby changing (as the changed length and direction of the arrow indicates) the motion of the body. When we apply a force to a heavy object we feel it within our own bodies; when we drive animals to do the same we see the exertion of their muscles and the strain on their tendons. But in inanimate nature (which is the particular concern of the physical scientist) it is only in a change of motion that a force can manifest itself. This is the very difficult and not at all obvious fact that has to be explicitly understood if a **mathematical model** of a moving body is to be constructed. The other, expressed in Newton's third and final law, is no more obvious; it is that when one body applies a force to another, the second applies the same force in reverse to the first—even though, for example, the cart being pulled by the bullock is not exerting itself.

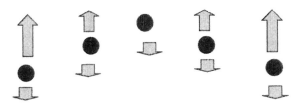

I would not presume to know whether it was the *general law* or the *application* of it to celestial motion that first formed itself in Newton's subtle mind. The question may even be logically meaningless but the next stage in our reconstruction must be an application to such workaday phenomena as the bob suspended from its spring. When the bob is forcibly removed from its rest position it is subject to two forces—the contending teams in our intuitive model—*viz.* the familiar and omnipresent one that tends to drag everything on earth down to the ground and another contained in the extension of the spring and tending to contract it. The first force is unvarying whilst its opponent pulls the harder the more the spring is extended. The drawing above represents the direction and magnitude of the forces in an intuitively simple way, suggesting how the advantage—which the Law tells us effects a change of motion—passes from side to side as the upward force decreases as the bob moves upwards releasing the tension in the spring. No more insight is needed to understand why the bob should oscillate nor—given only the genius of a Newton—is anything more than an elementary geometrical consideration required to understand the properties of orbital motion discovered by Kepler. To begin, were there no force acting on the moon she would move endlessly at unvarying speed in a straight line and (very surprising as this must seem) a line joining her to the earth would then sweep out equal area in equal times.

218

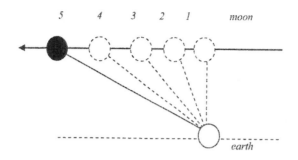

In the diagram above (which is adapted from Newton's *Principia*) the successive positions of the moon as a unit of time elapses are labelled *1, 2,* and so on. Having studies our Euclid we know that each of the triangles in the diagram with the earth at one vertex and the moon in two adjacent positions at the others (the triangles *earth-1-2* and *earth-2-3*) has the same area, they being on equal bases and between the same parallels, and so we see that this is so. But with the same sort of geometrical ingenuity that went into Euclid's diagrams Newton can also show that given any force on the moon directed always towards the earth, the same will still be true.

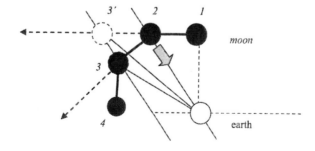

This time the diagram shows the position of the earth after successive infinitesimal intervals. As the first passes she moves from *1* to *2* in the diagram above and were there no force changing her motion towards the earth she would go on in the next to *3'*. However, given such a force (indicated by the broad arrow) she moves instead to *3*. Lines drawn between *3'* and *3* and between *2* and the position of the earth are parallel, so that the triangles *earth-2-3'* and *earth-2-3* are equal—and so also equal to *earth-1-2* which is the result Newton sought. Thus by merely considering a geometrical diagram to which the theorems of Euclid can be applied Newton shows that the motion empirically discovered by Kepler (the sweeping out of equal areas) is the intelligible consequence of the action of a force upon the moon directed towards the earth. Having constructed a rather complicated diagram, Newton is able to demonstrate with ingenious geometrical reasoning of the same kind that if this were an inverse square force, then, again as Kepler had observed, the satellite's orbit would be elliptical.

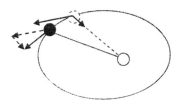

The drawing above should be compared with Kepler's: what was a mystery that could only be marvelled at as the arbitrary fiat of an inscrutable creator has become the consequence of a simple law. I have been at pains to stress throughout this essay that we understand only what we can picture, and a diagram like this is a new and very specialized crutch for our understanding. The understanding Newton's laws so far afford us of the behaviour of mundane and celestial bodies is merely *qualitative*. That, however, is not enough for the scientist: he wants to be able to make measurable *quantitative* predictions of their motions.

Mathematics being the science of quantities, *symbolization* is the next task for the model-maker: as was explained above this entails the production of *a drawing which has diagrammatic elements that also constitute the semantics of certain of the mathematician's symbols*. In the diagrams below the heaviness of the body— its *mass*, in Newton's terminology—is noted and velocities are represented by the arrows that are needed to suggest both a speed and a direction. The force is similarly represented by the arrow that is needed to suggest its magnitude as well as the direction in which it is applied.

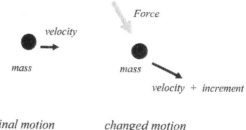

original motion   *changed motion*

Everything is now in place to permit the symbolic expression of the Laws of Motion. The elements that suggest themselves are the measured and directed arrows that give meaning to the mathematician's *vectors*. (Historically, of course, Newton as the pioneer he was, had to invent the mathematics he needed as he went along and this is the precise purpose for which he conjured up the vector.) The mass of the body is a quantity that has no direction and so can be represented by a letter, traditionally *m*, standing for a number. It labels the body under consideration in the drawing below in which its velocity and the force applied to it are represented by arrows labelled **v** and **F**, respectively.

$m (v + \Delta v)$

The incremental velocity of the body can be represented by using the mathematician's symbol Δv for the change in **v** as the force is applied. Since mv was the original *quantity of motion* of the body, the law requires the change in that quantity to be $m\Delta v$. The rate of change is that quantity divided by the incremental

221

time (Δt) during which the change occurs so that the vector equation that is the symbolic expression of Newton's Laws can now be written down: $\mathbf{F} = m\Delta v/\Delta t$. There is still nothing the scientist can do with his symbolic formula but that is changed when a graph of the position of a body is considered: the motion of the body if it is moving uniformly is now modelled by a particular straight line, and by a curved line (as in the example below) when it is changing; in either case its instantaneous velocity at any position *(i.e.* its speed measured in the same direction as its position) is the slope of the line at the corresponding point; the distance that body covers is the area on the graph beneath the curve, and when the slope of the graph is plotted as a separate graph, the slope this time is the instantaneous acceleration of the body. And, since the graph is the semantic basis of the calculus, in any case in which the motion can be represented by an analytic function all of these can be calculated by integrating or iteratively differentiating it. Our being able to *see* these things as we do in the graphs below is what gives its meaning to the symbolic version of the Newtonian laws. The space-time graph and its derivatives gives meaning to the terms "speed" and "acceleration" and relate them to "distance" but the other important intuitive term, "force," is as yet merely manifest in the changing slope of a curve; it too must be made visible if the original insight is to be applied.

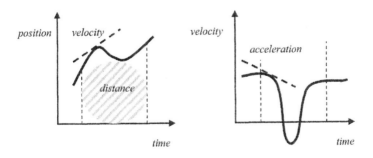

In the case of the bob suspended on a spring the specific insight required to understand its motion is that a suspended weight (like a knot at the middle of the rope used in a tug-of-war) is at rest when no net force is acting upon it. This case and countless others such as those of the ox-cart and the pendulum will have contributed to the emergence of Newton's great (if now, after three-and-a-half centuries, very familiar) insight that this is true of all movement in the world of our experience. This general insight into the essential sameness of movement in Nature enables the scientist in our reconstruction to go further with his investigation of celestial motion (or of any other specific case), for the next stage is the application—this time conducted entirely symbolically—of the *general* law to the *specific* case under consideration.

Here we resume our review of the Newtonian Paradigm.

(4) At this stage the original intuitive model has been transformed into something that the mathematician can show the scientist how to manipulate. In the case of the moon's orbit one vector, labelled r in the vector diagram below can represent the position of the moon in its orbit whilst another, F, can do the same for the net force exerted upon it.

An **hypothesis** *can now been presented in the form of this mathematical formula: F ~ r/r³ which the mathematical physicist could express in ordinary language as the suggestion that the force restraining the moon in its orbit (already known by Kepler's survey of Ptolemy's empirical data and Newton's geometrical argument to be a central one) is inversely proportional to the square of its distance from the earth. The further inspired guesses that this force acts between all gravitating bodies and varies with what he calls the gravitational mass of the body from which it somehow emanates lead Newton*

to postulate the symmetrical formula $Gmm'r/r^3$ as its symbolic expression. When he then calculates the fall of the moon in a month under the influence of this force, he finds that the distance corresponds to the diameter of her orbit. As this would be an astonishing coincidence were not its inertial and gravitational masses one and the same qualities of a material body, Newton finds it reasonable to identify the force that keeps the moon in her orbit with our familiar terrestrial gravity.

(5) The scientist's ultimate concern is with the concrete, material world that we apprehend with our senses (the empirical world). An hypothesis arrived at in the way just described must be tested empirically and to that end it must (much like the axioms in Euclid's original) allow theorems to be deduced. The form these must take is that of a prediction of measurements that might be made in the empirical world. For this reason the scientist must substitute for the vocabulary in which the model is specified the vocabulary of the world of our experience (much in the way the words of sailors have to be translated for landlubbers who then still lack the necessary knowledge of wind and waves fully to understand). He must talk about massive bodies rather than point masses and about velocities rather than vectors, and so on—about things which can be not only observed but also measured. A theoretical prediction that has been sufficiently corroborated becomes a **law of Nature** by analogy with, for example, geometrical law expressed by the Pythagorean statement concerning right-triangles.

The Syntactical Conception of Science

86. In their symbolic form Newton's Laws of Motion can be seen as the axioms of a system of deduction corresponding to a particular understanding of the Euclidean paradigm. This understanding—which neglects the model-building that, as we have seen, plays a crucial rôle in a more realistic analysis of Euclid's procedure—was the typical philosophical conception of Science in the Twentieth Century. It was variously known as "The Viennese View" of Science, or, in tribute to its predominant position, "The Received View" and was part and parcel of the philosophical movement known as **Logical Empiricism** (which had its roots in the intellectual community of Vienna before its dispersal by the Nazis). This name is appropriate, for its twin concerns were with, on the one hand, the *logical* relationships internal to a scientific theory and, on the other, the external relationship of the theory to the *empiricist's* world of observable, quantified experience.

The ultimate aim of the Logical Empiricists was to produce something like Euclid's *Elements* to be called the **Weltbild**[4]. This would unify not geometry but the whole of Science in one great axiomatic system. The construction of this edifice implied a demarcation of the bounds of Science, for anything that presumed to call itself "science" (as did Darwin's epoch-making theory of natural selection and Freud's culturally no less influential theory of the subconscious) but could not be accommodated to the scheme would thereby be disqualified as genuine science. To find its place in the scheme a theory would need to have two parts: first, the quasi-Euclidean component, an **axiomatic calculus** which would, like its original, be an intellectual construction, and, secondly, certain **rules of translation** which would establish a relationship between the calculus and the world of experience. In the perspective of Logical Empiricism these two components constituted the formal articulation of a scientific theory and were carefully distinguished from its application in the world of the data gathered by men of science.

It is the latter that is epistemologically fundamental, however, for although the theory makes no reference to experience it is only its success in explaining data already gathered (in "**retrodiction**," in the empiricist jargon) and in the **prediction** of the results of observations yet to be made that the theory is justified. Given his theories the activity of the scientist in seeking to understand the world

---

[4] *i.e.* "Picture of the world."

of experience reduces to offering explanations that accord with the so-called **Hypothetico-Deductive Schema** which relates observable events in this fashion:

> *observed event*
> *covering law*
> ___
> So: *predicted event.*

A **covering law** has the form *if (...a certain type of event, the* **cause** *...) occurs, then (...another type of event, the* **effect** *...) follows.* An event is subsumed (or "covered") if it is a token of the first type mentioned, and the law predicts the type of an event that subsequently occurs. Here is an example of the schema in which, in terms of the Euclidean paradigm, the "covering law" is an axiom of Newton's theory.

> *A force is being applied to this body.*
> *If a force is applied to any body, then that body will change its motion.*
> ___
> So: *This body will change its motion.*

The conclusion of the argument is hardly ambitious enough for the scientist: his whole purpose in reducing it to symbols is to enable a quantitative prediction to be made. The scientist substitutes specific observed values (expressed in standard units) in the symbolic translations of the natural language sentences, somewhat in this fashion.

> $F = m\,dv/dt$
> $F = 50; m = 10$
> ___
> So: $dv/dt = 5$

(Here the vector nature of F and v have, of course, been suppressed for simplicity of exposition.) What remains is to translate the now quantitative prediction back

226

into natural language: *this body will be accelerated by 5 standard units in the direction of the applied force.* This schema seems to the logical Empiricist to capture the scientist's predictions and retrodictions. We easily see how Newton's general theory of motion and his particular theory of gravitational attraction fit the bill with their application to the entire physical world: together they explain in retrodiction the insight extracted by Kepler from Ptolemy's data and similarly predict, on the basis of the perturbations of the theoretically expected orbits of certain planets, the existence of others never yet seen in the astronomer's telescope. ***Under the syntactical conception of science the locus of understanding is a text*** (which is what the little drawing below will be used to bring to mind when I need to return to this notion a little further on).

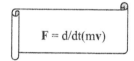

$$F = d/dt(mv)$$

Synchronic Critique of the Syntactical Conception

87. The characteristic tenet of this Viennese critique of Science was that scientific knowledge is sufficiently distinguished by the **meaningfulness** of what it says about the world. The test of meaningfulness is that the sentence should be capable of **verification**. A sentence would pass this test if an observation could be specified—one that might, at least in principle, be made—that would reveal whether or not the sentence were true. Sentences which fail to meet this criterion are easily composed, for example, "God created the world," "This picture is beautiful," "Rape is wrong," "The conjunction of Mars and Venus caused that damn to burst," "Giraffes have long necks in order to reach the leaves beyond the reach of other animals," "You have an unconscious desire to castrate your own father," and so on. In the epistemology of the Logical Empiricists a sentence will fail to be verifiable in this sense unless the non-logical words it contains are either the names of things we can observe, or else ultimately defined in terms of such names. We recognize the problems that the words and phrases "God," "wrong,"

"causes," "in order to," and "unconscious" pose for the empiricist and a little consideration shows that a very great deal of the interesting pronouncements that human beings might make about their world are, by this stringent standard, quite without meaning. In particular this is true of the whole of Philosophy of which nothing more appreciative should be said than "metaphysical nonsense."

The analysis of a scientific theory proposed by the Logical Empiricists accordingly supposes that the terms it employs can be divided into two separate vocabularies. The first of these, the **observational vocabulary**, consists of terms corresponding directly to measurements, such as the "position" of a body or the "time" at which an observation is made. The other, the **theoretical vocabulary**, consists of all the essential items by which this condition is not fulfilled. It would, then, in the case of Newton's theories, include both "mass" and "force." In order to meet the condition of verifiability, meanings are supplied for each theoretical item by a definition couched in terms of observational ones, whilst the semantics of the observational items themselves is supplied by detailing the operations by which they are measured. The definitions of the theoretical terms are specified in what are called **correspondence rules**; given that an applied "force" is what is manifest when a body changes its motion and the "mass" of the body in the degree of that change correspondence rules for Newton's theories would have to give their meanings to the *mass* of a body and to any *force* acting upon it by interpreting these notions in terms of its measurable *position, velocity* and *acceleration*.

Diachronic Critique of the Syntactical Conception

88. The notion of an axiomatic system is the content of the Logical Empiricist's *synchronic* critique of science, *i.e.* of what a science considered as an ideal, eternal entity ought to be. Euclid's laws of Geometry are verified not by experience but on the basis of logical proof. However, as has been explained, it is an empirical question (and so one to be resolved by experiment) whether the self-contained logical system of axioms and theorems that is Euclidean Geometry

correctly describes the space of our experience. What ultimately lies behind the Logical Empiricist insistence upon verification—*i.e.* upon the possibility of confirmation by experience—is the recognition that the laws of Science are not to be accepted without such confirmation. This is precisely because a correspondence between the self-contained logical system of a science conceived in the Euclidean manner and the world of experience can only be a postulate that is not itself part of the logical system. The laws it generates must be tested to see whether or not they agree with experience. The locus of prediction is the scientific experiment in which the relevant experience is artificially contrived. If the result is not in conformity with a proposed law, then the scientist must think again. This "thinking again" is an integral part of the scientist's procedure but one that is rather puzzling. It is the subject matter of what it is appropriate to designate the *diachronic* critique of Science, *i.e.* reflection upon how science ought to change through time in making progress towards its ultimate goal.

A law is only tested by an investigation (typically an experiment) whose result could reveal that Nature does not obey a law generated by the theory. Each time it passes such a test it has been **corroborated** (so that we have a little more confidence in it than we had beforehand) but our recognition of it as a law of Nature can never be more than provisional. The obvious reason for this is that the next experiment we devise might show the same law not to be followed. This is the insight behind the notion that the hallmark of a scientific theory is its susceptibility to **falsification**[5]. When it has been falsified, the rational response is simply to reject the theory and cast about for another which will *retrodict* what was actually observed to happen as the prediction failed to materialize. The new theory is then provisionally accepted in its turn until it is itself found to be at odds with experience. The further reason for the provisional status of all theories is the recognition of a creative aspect in our theory-making. This is usually expressed by saying that experience is not in itself enough to determine the content of the

---

[5] The notion is particularly associated with the name of Karl Popper (another Viennese but one with an uneasy relationship to his fellow).

theories we might suggest to explain it. This so-called **under-determination of theory by experience** means that different theories of the same phenomena can be expected to arise within any scientific community. When this happens it seems to Popper that a choice between them can be rationally made by considering the outcome of a **critical experiment,** *i.e.* an experiment deliberately contrived so that the results predicted by the two theories are incompatible.

Inadequacy of the Syntactical Conception

89. The first question that occurs in considering this articulated syntactical conception of science is whether the axiomatic method really is the only legitimate rational form of theorizing. To accept this claim would certainly be to reject as properly scientific the studies of biologists founded not upon anything that could be an axiomatic system but upon either morphological sketches and models or the structural map of a hideously complex molecule (with no bridge between the two); the studies of chemists founded (insofar as they are doing chemistry and not reducing their discipline to a branch of physics) upon the Periodic Table; or the therapeutic achievements of medical doctors founded upon patient histories; as well as a good deal of other activity that we are strongly inclined to regard as scientific. Whilst they could no doubt be reconstructed as quasi-Euclidean system simply by taking their results as axioms, it is not obvious that anything would be gained by doing so. More importantly the notion of the canonical status of an axiomatized theory can seem to misconstrue the intellectual content of Science, for insight is quite distinct from the organization of items of knowledge in a system of logical relations. Axiomatization can only be the result of exhaustive analysis and certainly brings elegant and economical order to an intellectual system as it clarifies it by revealing inter-connexions between the concepts it employs, but since the distinction between axiom and theorem is nothing more than an artefact of the organization it is not clear that it inevitably leads to the discovery of what is *fundamental* to the science. Mastery of such a system is nothing more than the ability *blindly* to draw the logical consequences

of what is already known; insight, on the other hand, is the essentially creative ability to *see* the novelty that it conceals. What is at issue, then, is whether what the scientist comes to know is the logical ampliation of what he already knows or something that can depend upon it in quite a different way. The Logical Empiricist must insist that no matter how we come to new knowledge, it is still only scientific knowledge to the extent it can be assimilated to an axiomatic system and ultimately to an all-encompassing *Weltbild*.

As we have observed self-reference is ever the root of perplexity and the meaningfulness of his own criterion of *meaningfulness* gives the Logical Empiricist some pause for thought. But it is the meaningfulness of the correspondence rules that is more significant for our own attempt at understanding what Science might be. Since theoretical terms are precisely the names of things not susceptible to observation, these rules cannot themselves be the deliverances of experience: it is clearly not experience that teaches us that in observing a change of motion we are measuring a force and a mass—for these things exist only as intellectual constructs and not as features of our experience. That is to say, they are not found by us in the material world but are, rather, part of the model which Newton created to represent it—and models (which have been our principal concern throughout this essay and will continue so to be) have no place in the *Weltanschauung* of Logical Empiricism. Without its correspondence rules no axiomatic system could be a scientific theory at all (since it would not then be about the world of our experience). But if, as is clearly the case, these rules are something adjoined to the logical system and not an integral part of it, then Science is not exclusively a system of logical relations after all.

Science cannot be conceived as a logically directed enterprise. Popper may have suggested a rational trajectory for its evolution, but Pierre Duhem had already described its progress in a rather more realistic manner[6]. He saw that the scientist's reaction to an unsuccessful experiment intended to corroborate his theory is no more determined by the failure than his theory is determined by

---

[6] Duhem's *magnum opus, La théorie physique: son objet, sa structure*, was published in 1905.

experience alone; he saw that the insight that we have identified with model-building throughout this essay is at least as highly valued by the practising scientist as is its not-yet-having-been-falsified. For Duhem, then, the rational response to the predictive or retrodictive failure of a law is not to abandon the theory but to review the entire complex of ideas of which it is just one part. This is the *holism* of the modern diachronic understanding of science. In Duhem's memorable figure our situation is not that of the watchmaker who has only to open the case and find the one cog or spring that is broken; it is more that of the physician whose sick patient displays the symptoms he does. Falsification is never, for the scientist, a *reductio ad absurdum*; he is not told where he has gone wrong: it may be in his initial *observations*; it may be in the theoretical *interpretation* from which they derive; it may be in the choice of *intuitive model* (in that unremarked disanalogies outweigh all analogy, making the seeming *insight* it provides mere illusion); it may be in the *calculation* that led to the theorem, or in the *translation* that produced the empirical law. Or it may be in the *logic* by which we performed the calculation, or even, finally, and most devastatingly, in the *human language* whose logic that is and in which the whole project was conceived.

The Semantic Conception of Science

90. In the perspective of the Received View Science is the business of making theories each of which is, like a theorem of Euclid's, a *text*. But our speculative reconstruction of Newton's procedure was intended to make clear that there is more to his theory than just its linguistic formulation and that the text may not even be what is essential to it, for it can seem that the Logical Empiricist's neglect of the rôle of modelling in science is at the very least a glaring omission. The notion that the scientist draws the logical consequences of laws which play the rôle of Euclidean axioms and then confronts these consequences with experience (as Popper and his followers would have it) is hardly realistic; what is done by the scientist who encounters a problem of motion in the material world is to use

Newton's law as the starting point for constructing a model of the phenomenon that interests him. Thus the use a scientific worker has for these laws is that of a paradigm for him to follow in his own work. Talk of the "paradigm[7]" of some given scientific field indicates one of possibly several characteristic ways of approaching the solution to problems in that field. More specifically *a paradigm is a particular style of model construction.*

The phenomenon in question might be a celestial orbit, the falling of an apple, the trajectory of a missile, the oscillations of a spring or a pendulum, the formation of waves on the surface of the sea or the propagation of light through empty space. In each of these cases acquaintance with the paradigm suggests a path to understanding. It suggests, on the lines demonstrated above, the sort of intuitive model (the conker whirled on a string, the tug of war, and so on) that will enable an original empirical intuition to be transformed into a mathematical model whose elements can then be seen as related by the law in its mathematical form. And this makes it possible to say quite precisely what it is to conceive of a scientific theory as a semantic entity: *under the semantic conception of science a theory is an ensemble of models.* It is when each of these models is thought of as a *token* of one and the same *type* that the theory emerges as some expression of that type.

In our discussions of the meaningfulness of words (and so of sentences) I stressed how although *something* was already present in its confrontation with a bison to the animal that became human, some representation in, say, the form of the schematic drawing "🐂" was prior to the presence of bison *qua* bison in his world of things, *i.e.* as things of a type of their own with which he might learn to cope. In somewhat the same way as the scientist contemplates flying arrows, and swinging pendulums the material world is in motion but it is only when the schematic picture that is a diagram displayed earlier and now repeated below has

---

[7] In Twentieth Century philosophy of Science the term "paradigm" was particularly associated with the name of Thomas Kuhn. He has been much criticized for not employing it consistently. The reader should not assume that its use in the present text coincides with any of his various uses for it.

been drawn that the scientist is in the presence of forces manifesting themselves as changes of motion with which he can reckon.

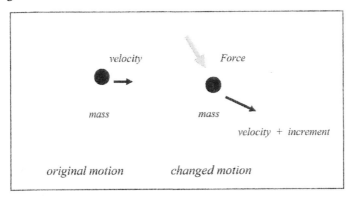

We can hardly know how many of what we should now consider to be its applications Newton may have considered before writing down the linguistic text or the symbolic formula which give expression to his theory, but in the perspective of the Semantic Conception of Science the intuitive models that are the individual bases of these applications are logically prior to the articulated theory and in that sense are what is fundamental to it. The theory having emerged from the ensemble of models, future models are tokens of the Newtonian type, so that we can also recognize a *mutual dependence of models and paradigm*.

The reply to the Logical Empiricist suggested by all this is that the diagram above which (1) is an abstraction that can be realized as the intuitive model of any phenomenon of movement in the material world, and (2) is composed of elements that can be incorporated into a mathematical model has a far clearer title to be considered Newton's theory than the text of any law. And, with a nod to Duhem, the reply to Popper similarly suggested is that *no experiment could ever falsify anything more than a token of the theory* and so certainly not the theory itself. The scientists who seem to their colleagues to be doing worthwhile science adopt a paradigm and may continue to use it as long as it generates *interesting* token theories in an expanding region of enquiry.

Kuhn, who was alongside Popper the most respected theoretician of Science in the Twentieth century, rejects the Popperian notion of a rational evolution of Science. In his irrational perspective—which is in terms of psychological and sociological impulses rather than logical motivation—scientists also abandon an established and well corroborated paradigm (by which he usually means either a "disciplinary matrix" or else an "exemplar" of good practice, carefully studied by recruits to the scientific community to be a guide to their future practice) in the advent of another which encompasses novel phenomena, particularly if it also seems to include the old by reducing it to a part of itself. Even when the predictions of a theory do fail scientists will pathologically hang onto it until they and their equally benighted colleagues are collectively forced by the catastrophe of accumulating failures reluctantly to adopt another.

Whilst many have found this less implausible than Popper's rational scenario of crucial experiments and immediate wholesale rejection of one theory and exclusive adoption of another it should be acknowledged that, in point of fact, paradigms exist alongside one another. This is indeed the case with Newton's theory which is not the only paradigm for the scientific study of the motion of material bodies (not even the only non-relativistic one), for there is a elegant and powerful alternative which makes use of a very different account. The alternative is known as "The Principle of Least Action[8]" and is hardly comprehensible without rather more mathematical training than I can allow myself to assume here. It will be sufficient to note that it does not talk about forces and masses moving through the space of human experience but rather about what is going on in another space, one quite impossible to visualize but known, for what this piece of intelligence may be worth, as *Configuration Space*. This is a space whose dimensions correspond to the possible positions and velocities of all the elements of some closed system. What it concerns is the properties of the *trajectories through* this space that correspond to the evolution of the system through time. So much will sufficiently indicate how very different this elegant and mathematically

---

[8] It is associated with the names of the mathematicians Legrange and Hamilton

powerful alternative is to Newton's theory. And this is what is of great significance, for the two are nevertheless *equivalent* in the sense that the symbolic predictions derived in either can also be derived in the other. It is tempting, then, to identify the theory of mechanics neither with Newton's theory nor with Legrange's but rather with a certain abstract entity that, as it were, somehow stands behind them both and behind any other equivalent theory that might one day come along. We must now recall the sense in which the mathematician uses the term "model" to designate some object that interprets a system of axioms, for in that sense both Newton's Laws and The Principle of Least Action can be seen as formulating models of what ought to be regarded as one and the same scientific theory. To see the situation in this light is to understand by "scientific theory" the not-yet-represented-entity of which the two are, in the sense now intended, different models. *Under the Semantic Conception Science an ensemble of models is the locus of scientific understanding.*

The Syntactico-Semantic Conception of Science

91 It might perhaps afford some satisfaction to the shade of Hegel, that great German thinker in deriding whom for his bombastic obscurity and rhetorical form of argumentation analytic philosophers in the English-speaking world can always win applause, to find me following his characteristic scheme of the evolution of philosophical explanation. This scheme begins with a *thesis*—which in our case would be the Syntactical Conception of scientific theory—and considers this in conjunction with an *antithesis*—here the Semantic Conception—to uncover their *synthesis*, the deeper reality of which these can be seen to be complementary aspects. We found our thesis to be lacking in an account of the rôle of insight in scientific understanding, and must now also concede that there is no less dire a deficiency in its antithetical rival. What the Syntactical Conception does explain—insofar as the logical properties of natural language can be assumed—is the ampliation of knowledge. Given this assumption nothing more than the syntactical entity (the text) is needed to produce this verbal argument:

"The rate of change of the quantity of motion of a body varies as the force applied to it. The gravitational force applied to one body by another varies directly as the mass of that body and inversely as the square of the distance between them. So, the acceleration of a body caused by another varies directly as the mass of that body and inversely as the square of its distance away."

But this is all that is explained, for even the symbolic application of the theory, perhaps in this form,

$$\mathbf{F} = d/dt\,(mv)$$
$$\frac{\mathbf{F} = Gmm'r/r^3}{dv/dt = Gm'r/\,r^3},$$

requires a mathematical model which itself can only be derived, in the manner demonstrated above, from an intuitive one. An understanding of a scientific theory as a purely syntactical object leaves us without any understanding of what the established relationship is between the world of experience and human symbolization—the relationship that, as we have seen, goes by way of the construction of models. On the other hand, our account of the Semantic Conception has shown how (in the example we studied) a sensory experience mediated only by natural language is, in the psychological event of insight, the occasion of the construction of a model. What is then lacking in this conception is an understanding of how a linguistic description of the model—extended, as it typically is, into a symbolic mathematical one—can enable an analogical manipulation of the content of the modelled experience to issue in predictions concerning further experience.

We see that a plausible theory of Science will require the subsumption of both the Syntactical and Semantic Concepts in an Hegelian synthesis. This synthesis is the Syntactico-Semantic Conception whose content can be explained as follows. Our acquisition of language makes present to us a world of named entities and types of events involving them. We understand the ordinary and commonplace amongst these events in the sense that they are the parts of a linguistic account of our experience which is coherent in respecting, as it does, certain intuitions that we recognize as *logical*. We seek to understand an event that is not yet part of this account by finding an analogy between it and something—a *model* for it—that is. We then talk about the model and in so doing—by virtue of a scheme of translation between the two—talk about the modelled event. The interesting, novel things we then find ourselves saying are *hypotheses* concerning the not-yet-understood subject of enquiry. The *insight* manifest in the construction of the model is justified to the extent the hypotheses it gives rise to can be assimilated to the account of our experience.

What distinguishes the general results of this process from scientific understanding is that in the case of Science the model is to a higher degree apt for transformation into a symbolic text so that the logical entailments of its hypotheses can be determined mechanically within a trusted artificial system and the predictions founded upon the model cannot be in doubt. In the scientific procedure the insight that informs a model whose hypotheses are corroborated is allowed to inform the construction of models of other unexplained events. An *ensemble of models* generating hypotheses that might be tested in this way is itself the model (in the mathematical sense) of a scientific theory and a linguistic expression of its essential features is a putative scientific *law*.

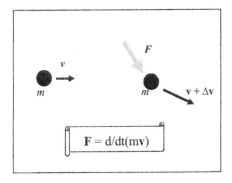

Under the Syntactico-Semantic Conception Science consists of ensembles of models systematically correlated with symbolically articulated laws. This is what the drawing above is intended to suggest in the case of Newton's theory. The objection to be expected to this conception of Science from advocates of the Syntactical Conception is that nothing in it other than the syntactical object is essential to that text which must be distinguished from heuristic aids to its composition or psychological aids to its application. This is sufficiently rebutted by considering whether the construction of models is independent of the mere linguistic understanding of a text. My purpose in beginning this essay with an explanation of the semantics of everyday language was precisely to make clear that understanding any text is in some sense the construction of a non-linguistic representation of some feature of experience. To feel we have understood a text is precisely to have constructed some such representation. But the form of that representation is not a matter of indifference: one is not necessarily as good as another. An adequate representation of the text of a scientific theory will, as we have indicated, have a certain *Protean* quality permitting it to become the secondary representation of many different intuitive ones which are thereby united as the various tokens of a single type. The construction of such representations is to some extent at least a matter of *tradition*: it is what is *taught* to students of science and what would only be recovered by a special effort were the tradition lost and only the text remained.

The no less obvious objection to be expected from advocates of the Semantic Conception is that the text is merely a contribution to a *systematic organization* of scientific knowledge that is nothing more than a supplement to the understanding that resides in the ability to represent the world of experience by appropriate models. The rebuttal this invites is that no representation tells us of itself what is intended to be done with it. This has been sufficiently stressed above in the case of "pictures" in the everyday meaning of the term.

Demarcation

92. The tentative conclusion of this essay is that the Syntactico-Semantic Conception properly captures the nature of Science. The obvious first test to which this theory should be subjected is that it succeeds in demarcating the province of Science in accordance with our pre-theoretical intuition of what Science is, *i.e.* that, on the one hand, it recognizes as sciences not only the Mathematical Physics that has been the model for its derivation but also Chemistry and Biology whilst, on the other, rejecting Astrology as being unscientific and enabling a principled decision to be reached in the cases of Psychology, Psychoanalysis, Economics, the Social Sciences and the Humanities. A criterion should also emerge for distinguishing scientific activity from Engineering.

An application of the present theory looks for the reduction of empirical intuition to a symbolic model. As we have seen the symbolic system in question in the case of Physics is that of Mathematics. This choice reflects its function which is to permit the logical derivation of laws with an application in the physical world which is the concern of the physicist. If Chemistry is to be recognized as a scientific enterprise then it is this function of the symbolic model rather than any mathematical provenance that will have to be insisted upon. Chemistry is concerned with the outcome of allowing different substances to interact with one another. As we recalled above the Chemist identifies certain structural formulæ with the substances which attract his attention. Each of these is derived from his atomic model of its molecules which itself is the deliverance of insight. The great virtue of these formulæ is that they allow the chemical equations which the layman particularly associates with this science to be written down. Thus the combustion in the atmosphere of carbon monoxide gas which is found to result in the production of carbon dioxide is represented as the *chemical equation* $2CO + O_2 = 2CO_2$. The balancing of the numbers of atoms of carbon and of oxygen, respectively, on the two sides of the equation represents the material consistency of such a reaction whilst the structural models of the molecules involved with their different types of bonds tell the chemist that the reaction is also possible. Whilst his knowledge of the constraints upon reactions is encapsulated in the Periodic Table, the layout of this table can only be explained by the physicist. This circumstance reflects the dependency of Chemistry as one more sub-discipline of the Natural Sciences but it clearly satisfies our requirements in its own right, for it is by considering his symbolic formulæ that the chemist makes the predictions which laboratory experiments can then corroborate. All of this is in conformity with the conception of Science being canvassed here. In particular, *pace* partisans of the Syntactical Conception, the locus of the chemist's understanding is the structural models with their bonds multiplied and oriented in space which can be drawn or imagined bursting apart and reforming, whilst, *pace* those of the Semantic Conception, the calculation that leads to the conclusions that can be empirically tested is found only in the equations.

What we find when we turn to Biology is, however, considerably less clear. Three very different insights seem to inform the thinking of the biologist. First there is the Darwinian *Tree of Life* which can easily be modified—as it routinely is—to accommodate any emerging morphological analogy amongst organisms; secondly there are the Mendelian factors of inheritance (or *genes,* in modern parlance) which can be made to manifest their influence in contrived experiments; and, thirdly, the biochemical machinery that sees the growth of organisms as a process directed by details of the structure of certain giant molecules found in the cells of living tissue. What is clear is that the study of the last component is an exercise in Chemistry, so that if the biochemists investigating this machinery are not scientists in virtue of being biologists, they nevertheless are in virtue of being chemists. The justification for identifying segments of DNA as genes can only be that the genetic material extracted from different organisms can be arranged in an evolutionary tree whose nodes and leaves can be correlated with those of a version of Darwin's original. What is troubling for the philosopher of Science is that this correlation must appear *miraculous*: whilst the chemist may understand how one codon encodes an amino acid and even how a sequence of codons encodes a protein, he cannot even begin to show us how a strand of DNA could encode an earthworm, far less a human being with all its individual anatomical details. Whereas we have no difficulty in seeing *the chemistry in our physics*, we neither see *the biology in our chemistry* nor even, indeed, any prospect of this ever being revealed. The reason for this is that we feel the processes of life to be something of a completely different nature to the mechanical processes of classical physics (and here the "classical" is of significance). Darwin's achievement that so startled his contemporaries was to eliminate the supernatural from the existence of highly evolved living things; however, it does not escape his careful reader[9] that he found himself ineluctably drawn to giving an important rôle to what he called "sexual selection" by which the females of a species, guided, one can only suppose, by some (typically very bizarre) æsthetic sensibility that is anything other than the mechanical interaction of blocks of inert matter, seem to *design* its males for their own extravagant delight. Biology is more than the botany that merely describes specimens of living things and arranges their dead remains in carefully organized collections, for it does have its principles—the *evolutionary unity* of all extant living things, for example, the *homeostasis* of life at all its levels, and so on—but these have the character of guiding dogma rather than of axioms from which deductions might be made.

Engineering

93. The designation "Genetic Engineering" is very apt, for whilst the molecular biologist can learn the biological consequences of tinkering with the chemical constituents of a cell or anticipate the medical prospects for an organism whose cells carry an observed abnormality, he is in the situation of any other engineer. The pre-theoretical distinction here—one that has been crucial for our whole argument—is between a theoretical and a practical discipline: the difference, then,

---

[9] q.v. the fascinating second part of his *The Ascent of Man.*

between *doing* and *understanding* that we attributed to the Egyptian builder and the Greek sage, respectively. Here we see the difference between a cook (whose cakes are liable to be the best) and a chemist but the engineer does seem rather more like the chemist than the cook. The engineer, but not the cook, may well treat the experience he obtains from his practical doing in a manner that we would nevertheless be inclined to admit as *scientific*, but there remains a difference which we must now uncover. Wherein does it lie?—Clearly, the task of the engineer is to get something done. To this end he may borrow *insight* from the scientist and puts it to work. More particularly he may borrow an intuitive model from the scientist and transform into a *working model* of the *engine* (which may be a bridge, a temple, a machine, a plant, a reactor, a spaceship, a bomb, a robot, or even a monstrous living organism) that will do the practical thing that he has in mind.

When the engineer borrows a model from the scientist, he does so because his own experience shows him that this will guide him to the construction of a successful engine. That pragmatism—and not the logical warranty that the scientist offers—is what may make science valuable to the engineer. Whilst the scientist's intuitive model (in being itself the material object it is) guarantees its own coherence his work has also its syntactical moment. What the text of his theory must accomplishes is to make clear (as does the title of a picture) how the model is to be *seen*. And here is the difference we are looking for: *the scientist's models are contrived to be transformed into symbolic models whose purpose is to secure by logical means the coherence of the text that describes what is to be seen in the model that informs them.* The scientist, then, goes on from what thereby becomes a semantic expression of his original insight to its syntactical expression. The engineer passes essentially from a material model to its material realization and so is interested rather in an expression of the same insight that might also be termed semantic.

But the splendid and emphatically pre-scientific engineering achievements of the Egyptians, not to mention the Romans, remind us that the engineer need borrow nothing at all from Science. He may rather produce an original model of his own in the *research* phase of his procedure, and transform it into something that works well enough for the task in hand in its *development* phase; through both of these his activity is like that of a scientific worker but any text he produces is more of the nature of the cook's recipe (with its varying quantities of ingredients for different numbers of guests). There is, of course, much insight involved in getting through all this but it is of a different kind to that of the scientist, concerning as it does *how stuff has to be handled* in order to get something done, rather than *what stuff shows itself to be when it is watched and probed*. The genetic engineer exploits a chemical model of the cell; the organisms he engineers will be the empirical phenomena from the study of which Biology may emerge as the science its practitioners intend it to be. It is because of this intention of theirs that we do not hesitate to say that these botanists and engineers already are scientists.

Creative Nexus

94. In distinguishing (as we did at the beginning of this essay) Occultism and Scientism the unmistakably occult force that holds the moon in her Newtonian orbit around the earth gave us pause for thought. The occult quality of the force of Gravity is a reflection of its non-mechanical nature: it seems as magical as the influence to which the astrologer is attuned of the stars upon our planet. This challenge was put to Newton by his own contemporaries and his splendid reply rings down the centuries: "Non fingo hypotheses." I take it that what he meant by this was that it was none of the scientist's business to explain why the mathematical model of the heavens works as perfectly as it does; it was enough to have constructed the model and seen the theory based upon it corroborated in all its predictions. This, of course, is very congenial to a proponent of the Syntactico-Semantic Conception for whom the model is the primary locus of understanding.

But by what principled means are we then to exclude Astrology from the province of Science?—It does seem to conform to the Conception with its *empirical intuition* of the revolving constellations and wandering planets; with its *intuitive model* of a divided circle; with its *mathematical model* of trigonometrical relationships between points on a circle; with its *rules of correspondence* between, on the one hand, planets and constellations and, on the other, personalities and moral qualities. What must be recognized, however, is that what makes a theory unscientific is not the *character* of the model but rather that of the *correspondence* between model and empirical reality. I certainly do not exclude the possibility that the pronouncements of an astrologer might be pregnant with profound wisdom and so an excellent basis for successful action, nor that they might have been honestly composed by him as he contemplated an astronomically correctly cast horoscope. What I would insist upon, however, is that the horoscope could never have been more than merely the *occasion* for an exercise of the wisdom the man possessed anyway. His wise pronouncement could only be the result of a *creative* manipulation of the concepts symbolized in his diagrams, informed, no doubt, by an insight into events here below that given his experience and intelligence he might have arrived at unaided. In Newton's celestial mechanics creativity is certainly involved in producing an intuitive model that can become an appropriate symbolic one; however, there is no call whatsoever for creativity in applying the mathematical model to the world of experience: the meaning of the symbolic pronouncements of the theory is not open to interpretation, whereas the horoscope has no meaning without it.

Summary

95. In this final chapter earlier insight has been gathered together to make the case for the Syntactico-Semantic Theory of Science. The venerable *Euclidean paradigm* for systematic intellectual work was reviewed and in particular the notion of the *laws* towards the enunciation of which it is directed. The peculiar character of scientific laws as generators of *quantified predictions* was noted and attention then directed to the *Newtonian Paradigm* for scientific work. A revised conception of the scientific rôle of laws began to emerge when the initiation of the

paradigmatic process was identified as the construction of models on the basis of an insightful *empirical intuition* guided by some *general law*. Detailed consideration of Newton's own derivation of the Law of Gravity showed how a *mathematical model* was developed from an original *intuitive model* upon which the particular demand was placed that its own constituent elements should *correspond with elements of the semantic foundation of items in the mathematician's repertoire of symbols*.

The Mid-Twentieth Century *Syntactical Conception of Science* was next explained with constant reference to Newton's Laws of Motion. It was explained that under this conception a scientific theory is an *axiomatic system* on the lines of Euclid's geometry which has an *application* to the empirical world in virtue of certain *correspondence rules*. This theory was found to be inadequate because identifying a scientific theory with an axiomatic system misplaces the knowledge that is the content of Science properly understood. In that conception Science is a corpus of *texts* (the statements of its laws) and there is no essential rôle for the *model-building* that is revealed by a more realistic evaluation of Newton's procedure. The alternative *Semantic Conception of Science* of the Late-Twentieth Century was accordingly examined. Here model-building is of the essence for a theory is now conceived of as a semantic entity, *viz. an ensemble of models*. When each of these models is thought of as a *token* of one and the same *type*, the theory emerges as an expression of the type. Under this conception it is laws that no longer have any essential rôle to play in Science, so that it must be rejected in its turn for the same sort of one-sidedness as its rival. What emerges from all these considerations is the *Syntactico-Semantic Conception of Science* which this essay is intended to defend. Under this conception the essential rôles of both text and model are given their dues. Chemistry is recognized, as it certainly should be, as a scientific discipline as is Biology once its relation to Engineering has been clarified. And, again as things ought to be, Astrology is found not to be a scientific discipline because of the essentially *creative* (rather than *determined*) nature of its relationship to the empirical world. Only such a conception can explain the applicability of Science to the world of experience in making predictions about natural events. Its explanation is in terms of the *symbolic manipulation of empirical intuition.*

BIBLIOGRAPHY

The titles listed below will be found useful in pursuing the themes of the present essay. The author's own book explains the hieroglyphic model of language exploited throughout; Arnheim's book is a thoughtful exploration of iconic representation; Smart's book is a very good introduction to the notion of Weltanschauung; Heath's book covers in great detail all the themes from Greek mathematics discussed in these pages; the papers by Fauvel and his collaborator's will help to clarify the complicated relationship between Occultism and Scientism; Dieudonné's erudite volume will be of interest for the mathematical notion of the abstract group which is related to the conception of Science defended here, whilst Brown's very readable book explores many themes in the Philosophy of Mathematics that have been touched upon in this essay; Stillwell's challenging book can be read as a thorough review of the conceptual apparatus of Mathematics; Weyl's famous book is the standard account of the notion of symmetry; the papers in Suppe's book—and particularly his lucid introduction to the collection—present the Syntactical Conception of Science, whilst Giere and van Fraassen present in detail the Semantic Conception; Duhem's volume explores the notion of holism; Silver's delightful book is an insightful survey of the evolution of modern science; and in Feynman's book a scientist who has little respect for Philosophy makes a valuable contribution to

the philosophical understanding of Science for which I am much indebted. (The
foreign titles will also be found in English-language editions.)

Arnheim, Rudolf: *Visual Thinking.* London: University of California Press, 1969.

Brown, James Robert: *Philosophy of Mathematics.* London: Routledge, 1999.

Dieudonné, Jean: *Pour l'honneur de l'esprit humain.* Paris: Hachette, 1987.

Duhem, Pierre: *La théorie physique: son objet, sa structure.* Paris: Marcel Rivière, 1914.

Fauvel, John et al.: *Let Newton Be!* Oxford: Oxford University Press, 1988.

Feynman, Richard P.: *The Character of Physical Law.* London: BBC, 1965.

Giere, Ronald N.: *Science without Laws.* London: University of Chicago Press, 1999.

Heath, Sir Thomas: *A History of Greek Mathematics.* Oxford: Oxford University Press, 1921.

Roscoe, John: *The Picture Theory of Language.* New York: Mellen Press, 2009.

Silver, Brian L.: *The Ascent of Science.* Oxford: Oxford University Press, 1998.

Smart, Ninian: *Worldviews.* New York: Charles Scribner's Sons, 1983.

Stillwell, John: *Mathematics and its History.* London: Springer, 1989.

Suppe, Frederick: *The Structure of Scientific Theories.* London: University of Illinois Press, 1974.

van Fraassen, Bas C.: Laws and *Symmetry.* Oxford: Oxford University Press, 1989.

Weyl, Hermann: *Symmetry.* Princeton: Princeton University Press, 1952.

INDEX

Each entry refers the reader to one or more numbered paragraphs *in the text.*

John Roscoe

Dr. John Roscoe, Professor of Philosophy at the University of Stavanger, Norway; B Sc (St. Andrews), Mag Art (Oslo), Dr. Philos (Tromsoe). Books include *Logica Post-Moderna* (1994), *Ideography* (1999), *Iconic Communication* (2000), *Scenario* (2002), *Illustrated Lectures on the History of Philosophy* (2004), *Examen philosophicum stavangeriense* (2004) and *The Picture Theory of Language* (2009).